Pies & Tarts

Pies & Tarts

Bounty
Books

First published in 2010 by Bounty Books,
a division of Octopus Publishing Group Ltd,
Endeavour House,
189 Shaftesbury Avenue,
London WC2H 8JY

An Hachette UK Company
www.hachette.co.uk

Material previosuly appeared in *Hamlyn New Cookery Tarts and Pies* by Mary Cadogan, published in 1994 by hamlyn and *Tart*, published in 2004 by hamlyn

ISBN: 978-0-753718-95-7

A CIP catalogue record for this book is available from the British Library

Printed and bound in China

Contents

Introduction 6

Pastry Recipes 14

Monday to Friday 20

Special Treats 66

Just a Bite 104

Index 126

Introduction

There is something incredibly satisfying about making pastry. It is not just the feel of the pastry between your fingers, or the wonderful smell of baking wafting through the house. It is also that you are offering something completely home-made that you have taken time and trouble over, in an age when so many meals have to be put together in minutes, quite often from packets in the cupboards or freezer.

Utensils and equipment
Most cooks would agree that the secret of good pastry lies not in expensive gadgets but in having a cool, quick hand. However, there are a few items of equipment that are essential for making good pastry.

Scales: Getting the correct proportions of flour and fat (and sugar, when you are making sweet pastry recipes) is actually more important than the precise quantities of each.

Work surface: Pastry should be rolled out on a clean, cool, level surface that has been lightly dusted with flour. You can buy special boards or you may prefer to use a work top.

Mixing bowls: Always use a bowl that is large enough to comfortably hold all the ingredients you will be using. Having to transfer to a larger bowl halfway through a recipe can be both tricky and messy.

Measuring spoons: Ingredients are often given in teaspoons or tablespoons. All spoon measures in the recipes in this book are assumed to be level (1 teaspoon equals 5 ml while 1 tablespoon equals 15 ml). It is worth buying a set of measuring spoons so that you can measure accurately.

Sieve: Sift the measured flour or flours (and salt, if required) into the mixing bowl. This removes lumps and separates the grains so that the fat is more easily mixed into the dough. You will also need a sieve for dusting sweet tarts with icing sugar or cocoa powder. Hold the sieve to one side of the tart, then shake or tap it lightly as you move it across the surface to achieve a light, even covering. If you wish, you can lay a doily or stencil over the surface to create a pattern.

Food processor: A food processor can be used to make pastry quickly. It reduces the time you have to handle the dough, which can be helpful in hot weather. Take care not to overmix the fat with the flour, however. A few short bursts will allow you to judge the breadcrumb stage. You may find you need a little more water than if you are mixing by hand.

Pastry brushes: You will need a fairly broad brush for applying melted butter to sheets of filo pastry, for example, and a finer brush for more detailed work, such as applying glazes to small pastry decorations.

Clingfilm: It is important that the pastry is allowed to rest so that it does not shrink and become distorted when it is cooked. When you chill unrolled pastry, cover it closely with clingfilm or put it inside a plastic bag. When you have rolled out and lined the tart tin or tins, do not trim off the excess pastry until you have allowed the pastry to rest again.

Baking sheets: You can either lightly grease a baking sheet or use a sheet of greaseproof baking paper.

Tins and dishes: Tart tins with loose bases make removing pastry cases from the tin easy, but lined and greased tins can also be used. Small pastry cases can be cooked in small cake or muffin tins. Metal containers give best results.

Cutters: Small tarts can easily be cut out with a pastry cutter, and you will find a wide range of plastic and metal cutters in all kinds of shapes and sizes. Run the point of a sharp knife around an upturned saucer to cut out larger pastry circles.

Baking beans: Many pastry cases are baked blind – that is, they are wholly or partly cooked before the filling is added so that the liquid in the filling does not soak into the pastry. To prevent the pastry rising during the initial cooking, a circle of greaseproof paper can be put inside the pastry case and held in place by baking beans. Dried beans or lentils can be used, although they do not have as long a life as ceramic beans.

Making pastry

Pastry-making is not an esoteric art, but a matter of following a set of simple rules, the most important of which is to keep everything cool – hands, head, equipment and ingredients.

Choosing flour

Plain white flour is the best choice for most recipes, giving a light, crisp pastry. Self-raising flour gives a softer, sponge-like texture and should be used for suet crust. Wholemeal flour, or a mixture of half wholemeal and half white, can be used for shortcrust pastry, but it tends to give a heavy, crumbly dough, which can be difficult to handle. Puff, flaky or rough puff pastries are usually made with strong plain flour.

Choosing fat

The type of fat you use affects the texture and the flavour of the pastry. It should be cold, so only remove it from the refrigerator shortly before use to make it easier to handle. Butter, preferably unsalted, gives the best colour and flavour, but when it is used on its own it can be rich and oily. Margarine is good for colour but has an inferior flavour. Soft margarine should be used for fork-mix, all-in-one pastry only. Lard, or a good-quality vegetable fat, gives a good short, crumbly texture, but lacks flavour and colour.

Other ingredients

Water: Use as little as possible. Too much water can make the dough difficult to handle and the cooked pastry tough.
Always use cold or iced water. For shortcrust pastry you will need about 1 teaspoon of water for each 25 g (1 oz) of flour. If you are adding egg, use proportionately less water.
Sugar: Some rich pastries, including pâte sucrée, use a small amount of sugar to give a crisp texture and golden colour.
Eggs: Egg, usually only the yolk, is used to bind rich pastries. It also adds colour. Beat it lightly with a fork before adding it.

Pastry-making tips
• With the exceptions of choux pastry and suet crust, pastry
benefits from resting for about 30 minutes before baking.
Wrap the pastry in clingfilm to prevent it from drying out
and put it in the refrigerator.
• It is vital to preheat the oven thoroughly, particularly for
pastries with a high fat content, which should be cooked at a
high temperature for light, crisp results.
• Measure the right proportions of fat to flour, according to
the type of pastry. For shortcrust pastry, use double the
weight of flour to fat. Richer short pastries use a higher
proportion of fat to flour.
• Unless you are making choux pastry, keep everything,
including your hands, as cool as possible.
• When you are rubbing in fats use only the very tips of your
fingers to keep the mixture cool. Lift the fingers high and let
the crumbs run through them back into the bowl.
• When you are rolling out and shaping pastry don't handle it
more than necessary as this will make it heavy.
• Don't add the liquid all at once. Flours vary in absorbency,
and too much liquid can make the pastry heavy.

How much pastry?
Here is a rough guide to how much prepared pastry you will
need for different sizes of tart tin. This is for lining the base
of the tin only. If you are making a pie with a solid pastry top,
double the quantity.

Tart tin diameter	Pastry quantity
18 cm (7 inch)	250 g (8 oz)
20 cm (8 inch)	375 g (12 oz)
23 cm (9 inch)	425 g (14 oz)
25 cm (10 inch)	500 g (1 lb)

Using pastry

Don't handle pastry more than necessary and always roll it away from you, using light, even pressure and adding as little extra flour as possible, as too much can result in tough pastry.

Rolling out

Dust a cool work surface and your rolling pin lightly with flour. Roll lightly and evenly in one direction, always away from you, moving the pastry around by a quarter turn occasionally. Try to keep the pastry even in shape and thickness. Avoid stretching the pastry, which will cause it to shrink during cooking. Depending on the recipe, shortcrust pastry is usually rolled to about 3 mm (³/₁₆ inch) thick; puff pastry can be rolled slightly thicker, to about 5 mm (¼ inch).

Lining a tart tin

Put the flan ring or tart tin on a baking sheet. Roll out the pastry to about 5 cm (2 inches) larger all around than the diameter of the ring or tin. Roll the pastry loosely around the rolling pin, use the rolling pin to lift it over the tin, then carefully unroll it into the tin.

Gently ease the pastry into the tin, pressing it into the flutes with your finger and taking care not to stretch it or leave air gaps underneath. Turn any surplus pastry around the edges outwards from the rim, then roll the rolling pin straight over the top so that the surplus pastry is cut and falls away, to leave a neat edge.

Baking blind

This is the process of part-baking pastry in the tin before the filling is added, to ensure crisp results. The pastry is weighted down to prevent it from bubbling up or falling down around the sides.

Line the tart tin with the rolled-out dough as usual and prick the base of the pastry with a fork, so that any air trapped underneath can escape rather than cause the pastry to bubble up. Place a square of nonstick baking paper in the pastry case and, taking care not to damage the edges of the pastry, half-fill the paper with dried lentils or beans or ceramic baking beans.

Bake as instructed in the recipe, usually for 10–15 minutes, then remove the paper and beans. Return the pastry case to the oven for about 5 minutes to crisp the base if necessary. Crumpled foil can be used instead of beans.

Using filo pastry

Filo pastry has a reputation for being difficult to handle, but if you follow these simple guidelines, you will find that it is no more difficult to use than any other pastry. To keep filo soft and workable, make sure that the pastry is covered all the time you are not actually working with it. Lay a sheet of clingfilm or a damp cloth ot tea towel over it or keep it wrapped, because it will become brittle and break easily if it dries out.

Work quickly, using up any broken or torn pieces of filo pastry between whole sheets – no one will notice. Do not moisten filo pastry with water, which makes the sheets stick together and disintegrate; keep the work surface dry for the same reason. Use fat, such as melted butter, to seal edges and to brush the pastry for crisp results.

Storing pastry

Freezing: Pastry is best frozen ready shaped, whether cooked or uncooked. Freeze pastry cases or pies in foil containers or freezerproof dishes. Empty pastry cases can be cooked from frozen; add an extra 5 minutes to the conventional cooking time. Filled pies are best defrosted before they are baked to ensure they are cooked through. Store for up to 3 months.
Rubbed-in pastry mix: Rubbed-in pastry mixture can be stored in the refrigerator for up to 7 days. Alternatively, it may be frozen for 3 months. Thaw before adding the water.

Pastry decorations

A modest decoration is part of the traditional look of pies and tarts. Leaves, a lattice and fancy edges all enhance their appeal and are very simple to make.

Pastry leaves

A decorative border of pastry leaves around the rim of a tart works particularly well on a tart with a smooth plain filling. Holly leaves make an attractive addition to Christmas tarts.

To make pastry leaves, pile any pastry trimmings on top of each other in a stack – do not press them into a ball, because they will rise unevenly. Roll the pastry out to about 3 mm ($^3/_{16}$ inch) thick.

Cut the pastry into long, narrow strips, about 2.5 cm (1 inch) wide. Make diagonal cuts across the strips to create diamond shapes. Press a knife gently against the pastry, taking care not to cut right through, to mark the veins on each leaf. Alternatively, roll out the pastry trimmings and use a leaf-shaped pastry cutter to cut out the leaves.

Arrange the leaves so that they overlap on top of the pie, securing them to the crust by brushing them underneath with a little water, milk or beaten egg.

Making a pastry lattice

A lattice of pastry looks attractive on both savoury and sweet tarts and pies. Keep the lattice strips well apart, leaving wide gaps to show the filling, or arrange them almost touching to make a closed lattice top.

To make the lattice, cut the rerolled pastry trimmings into long, narrow strips. Starting at one side of the tart, overlap the strips, weaving them alternately under and over each other, to make a wide trellis. Attach the strips to the edge of the tart by moistening each one with a little water and pressing it lightly in place on the crust. Trim off the excess pastry with a knife.

Making decorative edges

Plait: Cut three long, narrow strips of pastry. Pinch them together at one end and press this on the rim of the pie. Plait the strips around the edges of the pie, joining in extra lengths of pastry as necessary to go all around. Tuck the ends under.

Twist: Cut two long, thin strips of pastry and pinch them together at one end. Attach this to the pie rim and then twist the strips gently, arranging them around the pie edge as you go. Add extra strips, if necessary.

Flaking or knocking up: This is a technique used on pies with pastry-covered tops. It's important to seal the top and bottom layers of pastry neatly to prevent fillings from leaking out. Hold one finger lightly against the top of the pastry rim and press the blade of a knife horizontally into the cut pastry edge, making a series of shallow cuts. Do this all around the edge. This will also help puff and flaky pastry to rise.

Scallops: This decorative finish to a pie crust adds a professional touch and helps to firmly seal the edge of the tart. Place the knife blade at a vertical angle against the pastry edge and press your fingertip next to it on the rim. Make a vertical cut, pulling slightly upwards, to create a scallop. Continue around the edge at intervals of about 1.5 cm (⅝ inch) all around the tart.

Crimping: This is a quick and simple alternative to flaking and scalloping pastry edges. Push the finger of one hand into the top of the pastry rim. At the same time, pinch the outer edge with the finger and thumb of the other hand, pinching the pastry to a point. Continue crimping all around the edge of the pie.

Shortcrust Pastry

The classic choice for savoury and sweet everyday dishes,
shortcrust pastry is easy to handle and holds its shape well for
pies and tart cases.

Makes about 325 g/11 oz

200 g/7 oz plain flour
pinch of salt
100 g/3½ oz fat, such as equal quantities of butter and white
vegetable fat
2–3 tablespoons iced water

Sift the flour and salt into a bowl. Cut the fat into small pieces and
add it to the flour. Use your fingertips to rub the fat into the flour
very lightly and evenly until it begins to resemble fine breadcrumbs.

Sprinkle the water over the surface and stir with a palette knife
until the mixture begins to clump together.

Turn out the pastry on to a lightly floured surface and press it
together lightly with the fingers. Chill for 30 minutes before use.

Rich Shortcrust Pastry

The inclusion of an egg yolk gives a fine, crispy pastry that is ideal for sweet tarts but can also be used for savoury tarts if you need a standing crust.

Makes about 375 g/12 oz

200 g/7 oz plain flour
pinch of salt
100 g/3½ oz fat, such as equal quantities of butter and white vegetable fat
1 egg yolk
2–3 tablespoons iced water

Sift the flour and salt into a bowl. Cut the fat into small pieces and add it to the flour. Use your fingertips to rub the fat into the flour very lightly and evenly until it begins to resemble fine breadcrumbs.

Add the egg yolk and stir with a palette knife until the mixture begins to clump together. Add just enough cold water if necessary to make a firm dough.

Turn out the pastry on to a lightly floured surface and press it together lightly with the fingers. Chill for 30 minutes before use.

Pâte Sucrée

A sweet, enriched shortcrust pastry, this has a rich, biscuit-like texture suitable for sweet tarts and pastries. This recipe makes enough pastry to line a 20 cm/8 inch tart tin.

Makes about 375 g/12 oz

175 g/6 oz plain flour
pinch of salt
75 g/3 oz unsalted butter, slightly softened
2 egg yolks
1 tablespoon cold water
40 g/1½ oz caster sugar

Sift the flour and salt into a pile on a cold work surface and make a well in the centre. Add the butter, egg yolks, water and sugar to the well and use the fingertips of one hand to work them together into a rough paste. The mixture should resemble scrambled egg.

Gradually work in the flour with your fingertips to bind the mixture into a smooth dough. Press together lightly and form into a ball. Wrap in clingfilm and chill for about 30 minutes before use.

Puff Pastry

Well-made puff pastry will rise to about six times its height when it is cooked. Although it has a reputation for being difficult to make, the most important guideline is to keep all the ingredients cool.

Makes about 625 g/ 1¼ lb

250 g/8 oz plain flour
pinch of salt
250 g/8 oz cooled butter in one piece
1 teaspoon lemon juice
150 ml/¼ pint iced water

Sift the flour and salt into a bowl. Use your fingertips to rub in a quarter of the butter until it resembles breadcrumbs. Add the lemon juice and most of the water. Mix to a dough and gradually add the rest of the water to form a dry dough.

On a floured work surface knead the dough into a ball and flatten. Wrap it in clingfilm and chill for about 30 minutes.

Put the rest of the butter between two sheets of clingfilm and roll out to a square about 1 cm (½ inch) thick. Unwrap the chilled pastry and roll it out to form a square large enough to wrap round the butter. Put the butter in the centre of the pastry square and fold over the edges to encase the butter completely.

Dust the work surface and rolling pin and roll out the pastry to a long rectangle about 1 cm (½ inch) thick. Fold the bottom third on to the middle third, then fold the top third over the top. Rewrap and chill for 15 minutes.

Return the pastry to the work surface with a short edge facing towards you. Press down on the edges slightly then roll it out into a rectangle and fold as before. Repeat this six times, then chill the pastry. Roll it out to its final shape, then chill again for 30 minutes. 'Knock up' the edges (see page 13) so that the layers rise properly.

Cheat's Rough Puff Pastry

This deliciously rich and crisp, slightly flaky pastry is ideal for single-crust pies, pasties or sweet pastries. It does not rise as much as puff pastry, but it is far simpler to make.

Makes about 625 g/1¼ lb

250 g/8 oz plain flour
pinch of salt
175 g/6 oz butter, thoroughly chilled, until almost frozen
about 150 ml/¼ pint iced water mixed with
2 teaspoons lemon juice

Sift the flour and salt into a bowl. Holding the butter with cool fingertips or by its folded-back wrapper, grate it coarsely into the flour. Work quickly before the butter softens from the heat of your hand.

Stir the grated butter into the flour with a palette knife, then sprinkle with just enough iced water to start binding the ingredients into a dough. Press the dough lightly together with your fingertips.

Turn out the dough on to a lightly floured surface and roll it out into an oblong about three times longer than it is wide.

Fold the bottom third of the pastry up and the top third down, then press around the sides with a rolling pin to seal the layers together lightly. Chill for about 30 minutes before use.

Choux Pastry

This breaks all the rules for pastry making: it needs lots of heat and firm handling for good results. Use it for sweet or savoury buns, profiteroles, beignets and éclairs.

Makes about 500 g/1 lb

75 g/3 oz plain flour
pinch of salt
50 g/2 oz unsalted butter
150 ml/¼ pint water or equal quantities of water and milk
2 large eggs, lightly beaten

Sift the flour and salt on to a sheet of greaseproof paper. Place the butter and water in a saucepan and heat gently until the butter melts, then bring to the boil. Do not bring to the boil before the butter melts.

Draw the pan off the heat and immediately add the flour, all at once. Beat with a wooden spoon or electric hand mixer just until the mixture forms a smooth ball which leaves the sides of the pan clean. Do not overbeat at this stage or the paste will become oily.

Cool the mixture for 2 minutes. Gradually add the eggs, beating hard after each addition, and continue to beat until the mixture is smooth and glossy. The paste should be just soft enough to fall gently from the spoon. Use the pastry immediately or cover closely and chill until needed.

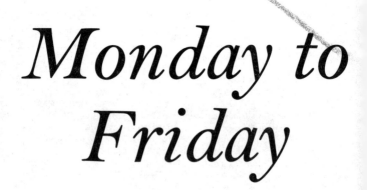

Monday to Friday

With the simple addition of a few steamed vegetables, pies and tarts make interesting and comforting midweek supper dishes. Or just serve them with a simple salad for a light lunch with friends.
The sweet pies and tarts featured towards the end of this chapter can be served as delicious deserts or tempting teatime snacks.

Goats' Cheese and Cherry Tomato Puff

Serve this delicious tart hot either as a starter or for a light lunch with a salad of bitter leaves. If possible, use a mixture of red and yellow tomatoes.

Serves 4–6

250 g/8 oz puff pastry, defrosted if frozen
2–3 tablespoons olive oil
250 g/8 oz cherry tomatoes, sliced
250 g/8 oz firm goats' cheese, sliced
2 teaspoons chopped thyme
salt and pepper

Roll out the pastry and trim to a 23 cm/9 inch round. Transfer to a prepared baking sheet and brush lightly with olive oil.

Spread half the sliced cherry tomatoes over the pastry to within 2.5 cm/1 inch of the edge.

Arrange the goats' cheese over the top and scatter with the remaining cherry tomatoes. Season with a little salt and pepper. Sprinkle with the thyme and drizzle 1–2 tablespoons of olive oil over the top. Bake in a preheated oven, 220°C (425°F) Gas Mark 7 for 20–25 minutes until the pastry is risen, crisp and golden-brown.

THYME

Aubergine, Tomato and Haloumi Tart

Haloumi is a creamy-textured, slightly sharp Greek cheese that goes particularly well with aubergine. If you can't find haloumi use mozzarella instead.

Serves 4

250 g/8 oz puff pastry, defrosted if frozen
beaten egg or milk, to glaze
1 tablespoon sun-dried tomato paste
375 g/12 oz aubergines, sliced
2 tablespoons olive oil
5 ripe tomatoes, sliced
125 g/4 oz haloumi cheese, thinly sliced
2 teaspoons chopped oregano
50 g/2 oz green olives, pitted and halved
salt and pepper

Roll out the pastry to a 25 cm/10 inch square and put it on a prepared baking sheet. Use a sharp knife to make two L-shaped cuts in the pastry 2.5 cm/1 inch in from the edges, leaving the two opposite corners uncut. Brush the edges of the pastry with water.

Lift up one cut corner and draw it across the pastry to the opposite cut side. Repeat with the other cut side to form a case. Brush the edges of the pastry with egg or milk and prick the base. Spread the tomato paste over the base of the pastry case.

Brush the aubergine slices with oil and cook under a preheated moderate grill until lightly browned. Turn, brush again with oil and brown on the other side.

Arrange the aubergine slices, tomatoes and cheese in the pastry case. Sprinkle with oregano and olives and season to taste. Bake in a preheated oven, 200°C (400°F) Gas Mark 6 for 25 minutes until the pastry is golden. Serve warm.

Roast Vegetable and Feta Tart

Feta cheese, the best known Greek cheese, is made from ewes' milk. Its distinctive flavour goes well with these Mediterranean vegetables. Serve warm or cold.

Serves 6

1 aubergine, sliced
1 red pepper, cored, deseeded and cut into thick strips
1 onion, cut into wedges
2 courgettes, cut into thick slices
3 tomatoes, halved
2 garlic cloves, chopped
3 tablespoons olive oil
4 small rosemary sprigs
125 g/4 oz feta cheese, crumbled
2 tablespoons grated Parmesan cheese
salt and pepper

Pastry
125 g/4 oz self-raising flour
50 g/2 oz oatmeal
75 g/3 oz chilled butter, diced
3 tablespoons cold water

Make the pastry. Mix the flour and oatmeal then rub in the butter. Add the water and mix to a firm dough. Knead briefly, then chill for 30 minutes.

Mix all the vegetables in a roasting tin. Add the garlic, oil and rosemary and season to taste. Turn the mixture to coat the vegetables evenly and roast for 35 minutes.

Meanwhile, roll out the pastry and line a 23 cm/9 inch tin. Bake blind in a preheated oven, 200°C (400°F) Gas Mark 6 for 15 minutes. Remove the paper and beans or foil and return to the oven for 5 minutes.

Fill the pastry case with the vegetables, arrange the feta on top and sprinkle with Parmesan. Return to the oven for 10 minutes.

Courgette and Red Pepper Tart

Serves 6

2 tablespoons olive oil
2 red peppers, cored, deseeded and chopped
375 g/12 oz courgettes, trimmed
2 eggs, beaten
300 ml/½ pint milk
50 g/2 oz mature Cheddar cheese, grated
salt and pepper

Pastry
175 g/6 oz plain flour
1 teaspoon paprika
75 g/3 oz chilled butter, diced

Sift the flour and paprika into a bowl. Add the butter and rub in with the fingertips until the mixture resembles fine breadcrumbs. Add enough cold water to mix to a firm dough. Turn out the dough on to a lightly floured surface and knead briefly. Chill for 30 minutes.

Roll out the pastry and line a 23 cm/9 inch pie dish. Cut the trimmings into leaf shapes and stick them around the rim of the tart with a little water. Chill the pastry case for 30 minutes, then bake blind in a preheated oven, 200°C (400°F) Gas Mark 6 for 15 minutes. Remove the paper and beans or foil and set the pastry case aside. Lower the oven temperature to 180°C (350°F), Gas Mark 4.

Heat the oil in a frying pan and cook the peppers gently until soft. Season to taste with salt and pepper and purée in a food processor or blender. Alternatively, press the peppers through a sieve. Cut the courgettes into ribbons. Cook them in a saucepan of salted boiling water for 2 minutes, then drain and refresh under cold water. Drain again and pat dry with kitchen paper.

Beat the eggs, milk and cheese in a bowl and season to taste with salt and pepper. Spread the pepper purée over the base of the tart. Arrange the courgette ribbons evenly over the top and pour over the cheese sauce. Bake for 25 minutes until the filling is set and golden.

Tarte au Fromage

This hot soufflé cheesecake is a variation of a classic French supper dish. The sauce can be prepared in advance – cover and chill until required. Serve the tart with a crisp green salad.

Serves 4

375 g / 12 oz shortcrust pastry
50 g / 2 oz butter
50 g / 2 oz plain flour
300 ml / ½ pint milk, warmed
250 g / 8 oz Lancashire cheese, grated
6 eggs, separated
2 tablespoons snipped chives, plus extra to garnish
1 tablespoon chopped parsley, plus extra to garnish
½ teaspoon Tabasco sauce or to taste
salt and pepper

Roll out the pastry and line a deep 20 cm / 8 inch loose-based cake tin. Chill the pastry case for 30 minutes, then bake blind in a preheated oven, 190°C (375°F) Gas Mark 5 for 15 minutes. Remove the paper and beans or foil and return the tart to the oven for a further 5 minutes. Leave to cool in the tin.

Melt the butter in a saucepan, blend in the flour and cook over a low heat for 2–3 minutes, stirring all the time. Gradually pour in the milk, beating continuously. Take off the heat and cool slightly.

Beat in the grated cheese and the egg yolks, one at a time. Return to a gentle heat and stir until the cheese has melted. Season to taste with salt and pepper and stir in the chives, parsley and Tabasco.

Whisk the egg whites in a bowl until they form stiff peaks and gently fold them into the cheese mixture. Pour the mixture immediately into the cooked pastry case. Bake in a preheated oven, 200°C (400°F), Gas Mark 6, for 30 minutes until well risen and golden. Carefully remove the pastry case from the tin, scatter chopped parsley and chives over the top and serve immediately.

Beetroot and Camembert Tart

Do not trim the roots of the beetroots too close to the top of the globe before cooking them, and peel them once cooked so that they do not lose their rich red colour.

Serves 6–8

25 g/1 oz butter
2 tablespoons honey
3 red onions, thinly sliced
300 ml/½ pint red wine
500 g/1 lb cooked beetroot, each beet cut into 6 segments
3 tablespoons chopped thyme, plus sprigs to garnish
375g/12 oz puff pastry, defrosted if frozen
150 g/5 oz Camembert, cut into wedges
salt and pepper

Melt the butter and honey in a large sauté pan. Add the onions and cook over a medium heat until soft. Add the red wine, season well with salt and pepper and leave to simmer until the mixture has reduced by at least half.

Add the beetroot and continue to simmer until the liquid is thick and glossy. Remove from the heat, stir in half the thyme and leave to cool slightly.

Roll out the pastry and put it on a prepared baking sheet. Use a sharp knife to score a line around the edge, about 2.5 cm/1 inch in from the sides; do not cut right through the pastry.

Spoon the filling on to the pastry making sure you don't go over the border mark. Scatter the cheese slices and the remaining thyme over the top. Bake in a preheated oven, 200°C (400°F) Gas Mark 6 for 20–25 minutes until the pastry has risen and the cheese is bubbling. Garnish with fresh thyme sprigs.

Sardine Tart with Chermoula

Make the chermoula before you prepare the pastry so that the
flavours of the sauce have time to develop.

Serves 4

375 g / 12 oz puff pastry, defrosted if frozen
$^1/_2$ egg, beaten
25 g / 1 oz breadcrumbs
5 sardines, heads, tails and backbones removed
1 beef tomato, halved and thickly sliced

Lemon chermoula
$^1/_2$ red onion, finely chopped
2 garlic cloves, crushed
3 small preserved lemons, pulp removed and finely chopped
grated rind of 1 lemon and 1 tablespoon of juice
4 tablespoons chopped coriander
4 tablespoons chopped parsley
1 teaspoon paprika
1 teaspoon cumin
$^1/_2$ teaspoon cayenne pepper
4 tablespoons olive oil
salt and pepper

Mix all the chermoula ingredients together in a bowl, season well
with salt and pepper then leave to stand. Roll out the pastry to 23 x
18 cm/9 x 7 inch rectangle and put it on a prepared baking sheet.
Use a sharp knife to score a mark all the way round the edge, about
2.5 cm/1 inch in from the sides; do not cut right through. Brush the
pastry with egg and bake in a preheated oven, 200°C (400°F), Gas
Mark 6 for 15 minutes until risen. Push down the centre piece
leaving the border intact. Brush the base of the tart with beaten egg
while the pastry is still hot.

Sprinkle the base with the breadcrumbs then spoon over half the
chermoula mixture. Arrange rows of sardines and sliced tomatoes
alternately down the length of the tart base.

Top with the remaining chermoula and bake for 25 minutes until
the sardines are cooked and the sides of the tart are golden.

Crunchy Fish Pie

Serves 4

300 g/10 oz shortcrust pastry
200 g/7 oz skinned cod fillet
200 g/7 oz undyed smoked haddock fillet
250 ml/8 fl oz milk
1 bay leaf
5 spring onions, chopped
200 g/7 oz shelled raw prawns
75 ml/3 fl oz double cream
25 g/1 oz plain flour
25 g/1 oz butter
3 tablespoons chopped parsley
salt and pepper

Crumble topping
25 g/1 oz butter
100 g/3½ oz coarse breadcrumbs
3 tablespoons chopped parsley

Roll out the pastry and line a 20 cm/8 inch tart tin. Chill for
30 minutes, then bake blind in a preheated oven, 200°C (400°F), Gas
Mark 6 for 15 minutes. Remove the paper and beans or foil and return
to the oven for a further 5 minutes.

Put the fish, milk and bay leaf in a sauté pan and bring to a gentle
boil. Simmer for 3 minutes, remove from the heat, cover with a lid
and leave until cold. Strain the liquid into a jug, discard the bay leaf
and set aside. Flake the fish into large pieces and put them in the tart
case with the spring onions and prawns.

Put the reserved milk and cream in a saucepan with the flour and
butter. Stir constantly over a low heat until the butter has melted.
Continue to stir until the sauce thickens. Allow to simmer for
2–3 minutes, then remove from the heat and stir in the chopped
parsley. Season well with salt and pepper and pour over the fish.

Melt the butter in a frying pan and gently fry the breadcrumbs
for 2–3 minutes until they are light golden in colour. Add the parsley
and spoon over the top of the tart. Bake the pie in the preheated oven
for 20 minutes until the top is golden and the sauce starts to bubble
around the sides. Leave to cool slightly before serving.

Quiche Lorraine

Although this famous dish is often made with cheese and onions, in the traditional recipe the pastry case is filled with bacon, eggs and cream. Serve the quiche warm or cold.

Serves 4–6

300 g / 10 oz rich shortcrust pastry
175 g / 6 oz rindless smoked back bacon
250 ml / 8 fl oz single cream
2 eggs, beaten
grated nutmeg
salt and pepper

Make the pastry (see page 15). Roll it out and line a 20 cm / 8 inch tart tin. Chill the pastry case for 30 minutes, then bake blind in a preheated oven, 180°C (350°F), Gas Mark 4 for 15 minutes. Remove the paper and beans or foil and return the pastry case to the oven for a further 10 minutes.

Grill the bacon until crisp, then drain it on kitchen paper and crumble or cut it into pieces.

Beat the cream and eggs in a bowl with the grated nutmeg and season to taste with salt and pepper. Sprinkle the bacon over the case and pour the cream and egg filling over the top.

Put the tart tin on a baking sheet and bake in the preheated oven for 30–35 minutes until the filling is just set and the pastry is golden.

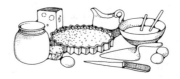

Mushroom Tart with Smoked Bacon and Thyme

When you are arranging the mushrooms, you may need to overlap them slightly so that they fit neatly. Serve warm with a tomato salad.

Serves 4

300 g/10 oz shortcrust pastry
5 large field mushrooms
2 tablespoons chopped thyme
2 tablespoons olive oil
250 g/8 oz smoked streaky bacon, chopped
1 onion, roughly chopped
3 eggs, beaten
200 ml/7 fl oz double cream
salt and pepper
thyme sprigs, to garnish

Roll out the pastry and line a 35 x 12 cm/14 x 5 inch fluted tart tin. Chill the pastry case for 30 minutes then bake blind in a preheated oven, 200°C (400°F), Gas Mark 6 for 10 minutes. Remove the paper and beans or foil and return the pastry case to the oven for a further 10 minutes.

Put the mushrooms in a roasting tin, sprinkle over half the chopped thyme and drizzle with 1 tablespoon of olive oil. Cook in the oven for 12 minutes, then remove and leave to cool.

Heat the remaining oil in a frying pan. Add the bacon and onion and cook over a medium high heat for 5 minutes until cooked and lightly golden. Spoon over the base of the tart.

Beat together the eggs, cream and remaining thyme, season to taste with salt and pepper and pour the mixture into the pastry case. Arrange the mushrooms down the centre of the tart, overlapping them slightly. Bake the tart in a preheated oven for 25–30 minutes until it is coloured on top and set in the centre. Garnish with thyme.

Lentil, Bacon, Spinach and Taleggio Tart

Taleggio is an Italian cheese, made from cow's milk. It has a pale pink rind and a soft, creamy texture.

Serves 6

300 g/10 oz shortcrust pastry
100 g/3½ oz red lentils
1 tablespoon olive oil
250 g/8 oz streaky bacon, chopped
225 g/7½ oz baby spinach
3 eggs
2 tablespoons sage, plus a few leaves for garnish
200 ml/7 fl oz crème fraîche
100 g/3½ oz Taleggio cheese, cut into cubes
6 cherry tomatoes, halved
salt and pepper
sage leaves, to garnish

Roll out the pastry and line a 23 cm/9 inch tart tin. Chill the pastry case for 15 minutes, then bake blind in a preheated oven, 200°C (400°F), Gas Mark 6 for 15 minutes. Remove the paper and beans or foil and return to the oven for a further 5 minutes.

Meanwhile, cook the lentils in salted boiling water for 10 minutes. Drain and leave to cool slightly. Heat the oil in a frying pan and cook the bacon for 6–7 minutes until golden and crisp.

Steam the baby spinach for 1–2 minutes, drain in a sieve and squeeze out as much liquid as possible using the back of a spoon. Roughly chop the spinach.

Fill the tart base with the spinach, bacon and lentils. Beat the eggs, sage and crème fraîche and season with black pepper. Pour into the tart and top with the cheese and tomatoes. Bake in a preheated oven for 40 minutes until the filling is firm. Garnish with sage.

Mediterranean Salami and Olive Tart

Use good-quality Italian salami in this recipe to give an authentic flavour of the Mediterranean. Serve the tart warm with a salad of fresh, crisp leaves.

Serves 4–6

250 g/8 oz canned chopped tomatoes
1 tablespoon tomato purée
2 teaspoons dried oregano
125 g/4 oz sliced salami
75 g/3 oz black olives, pitted
salt and pepper

Pastry
250 g/8 oz strong white flour
1 teaspoon easy-blend yeast
1 teaspoon salt
150 ml/¼ pint hand-hot water
1 tablespoon olive oil

Mix the flour, yeast and salt in a bowl. Add the water and oil and mix quickly to a soft dough. Turn out on a lightly floured surface and knead for 5 minutes. Put the dough in an oiled polythene bag, tie the top loosely and leave to rise for 30 minutes.

Combine the chopped tomatoes and tomato purée in a small saucepan. Add 1 teaspoon of the oregano and season to taste with salt and pepper. Bring to the boil, stirring, then lower the heat and simmer for about 5 minutes until thickened. Leave to cool.

Roll out the pastry and line a 33 x 23 cm/13 x 9 inch greased Swiss roll tin. Spread with the tomato mixture and arrange the salami slices on top. Sprinkle with the olives and remaining oregano.

Bake in a preheated oven, 220°C (425°F), Gas Mark 7 for 20–25 minutes until the pastry edges are crisp and golden brown.

Mexican Chilli Bean Tart

When you are removing the seeds and cutting the flesh of chillies, take care that you do not accidentally touch your lips or eyes, and wash your hands thoroughly afterwards.

Serves 6

300 g/10 oz shortcrust pastry
500 g/1 lb minced beef
1 onion, finely chopped
1 red chilli, deseeded and finely chopped
1 garlic clove, crushed
30 g/1¼ oz packet taco seasoning mix
400 g/13 oz can chopped tomatoes
4 tablespoons vegetable stock
400 g/13 oz can mixed beans, rinsed and drained
50 g/2 oz nachos, broken slightly
100 g/3½ oz Cheddar cheese, grated
2 tablespoons chopped coriander leaves

To serve
soured cream
tomato salsa

Roll out the pastry and line a 23 cm/9 inch fluted tart tin. Chill the pastry case for 30 minutes, then bake blind in a preheated oven, 200°C (400°F), Gas Mark 6 for 15 minutes. Remove the paper and beans or foil and return to the oven for a further 5 minutes.

Put the mince in a nonstick pan and cook for 5 minutes, stirring to break up the lumps of meat, until it is evenly browned. Add the onion, chilli, garlic and taco mix and continue to cook for 2–3 minutes. Add the tomatoes and stock and season to taste. Bring to the boil and simmer for 10 minutes. Stir in the mixed beans and cook for a further 2 minutes until the sauce thickens.

Pour the sauce into the tart case. Mix together the nachos, cheese and coriander and put them on top of the sauce.

Bake in the preheated oven for 20 minutes until the cheese has melted and the nachos have coloured. Leave to stand for about 15 minutes before serving with soured cream and tomato salsa.

Italian Sausage and Onion Tart

Keep the paper-thin sheets of filo pastry covered with clingfilm
or a damp cloth until you are ready to use them, to prevent
them from drying out.

Serves 4

3 tablespoons olive oil
6 Italian sausages
2 red onions, cut into wedges
6 sheets filo pastry
100 g/3½ oz mascarpone cheese
50 g/2 oz Roquefort cheese
3 large eggs
2 tablespoons milk
1 tablespoon wholegrain mustard
chives, to garnish

Heat 1 tablespoon of the oil in a frying pan and cook the sausages
and onions over a medium heat for about 15 minutes until they are
browned and cooked. Leave to one side.

Brush the filo sheets with the remaining oil. Line a 35 x 12 cm/
14 x 5 inch loose-based tart tin with the pastry, overlapping and
overhanging the sheets. Bunch up the overhanging filo to make a rim
around the sides. Bake in a preheated oven, 180°C (350°F), Gas Mark
4 for 10 minutes or until the base is dry. Leave the oven on.

Whisk together the mascarpone, Roquefort, eggs, milk and
mustard to make a smooth mixture. Pour it into the base of the tart.

Arrange the sausages and onion wedges evenly over the batter.
Bake for 30–35 minutes until golden and set. Serve warm, garnished
with fresh chives.

Potato and Salami Tart with Red Pesto

Ready-made pesto in a range of flavours and colours is widely available in supermarkets, but if you prefer, use your favourite recipe in this tart.

Serves 4

475 g/15 oz potatoes
300 g/10 oz puff pastry, defrosted if frozen
65 g/2½ oz ready-made red pesto
1½ tablespoons crème fraîche
75 g/3 oz salami slices
40 g/1½ oz melted butter

Cook the potatoes in a pan of salted boiling water for 20–25 minutes. Drain, leave them to cool, then cut them into 1 cm/½ inch slices.

Roll out the pastry to about 5 mm/¼ inch thick, put it on a prepared baking sheet and chill for 30 minutes. Cut the pastry into a 23 cm/9 inch disc and use a sharp knife to score a border about 2.5 cm/1 inch in from the edge all the way round; do not cut right through the pastry.

Mix the pesto with the crème fraîche and spread the mixture over the pastry, keeping inside the border. Arrange the potato and salami slices alternately over the pesto base.

Brush the tart with melted butter and bake it in a preheated oven, 200°C (400°F), Gas Mark 6 for 30–35 minutes until the pastry is risen and golden.

Sweet Potato, Chorizo and Red Pepper Tart

Chorizo is a Spanish pork sausage, traditionally flavoured with red peppers. It is a wonderful complement to the sweet potato.

Serves 4

750 g/1½ lb sweet potato, cut into 2.5 cm/1 inch cubes
1 large red pepper, cored, deseeded and cut into 2.5 cm/1 inch cubes
3 garlic cloves, left in their skins
2 tablespoons olive oil
150 g/5 oz chorizo, cut into 1 cm/½ inch cubes
125 g/4 oz ricotta cheese
100 g/3½ oz Cheddar cheese, grated
2 tablespoons crème fraîche
2 egg yolks
375 g/12 oz shortcrust pastry
1 egg, beaten, to glaze
3 rosemary sprigs
salt and pepper

Put the sweet potato, red pepper and garlic in a roasting dish. Drizzle with olive oil, season with salt and pepper and bake in a preheated oven, 200°C (400°F), Gas Mark 6 for 15 minutes. Add the chorizo and bake for a further 5–10 minutes or until the vegetables are slightly golden. Remove and leave to cool.

Push the garlic pulp out of the skins and put in a bowl with the ricotta, Cheddar, crème fraîche and egg yolks. Beat together to make a smooth mixture.

Roll out the pastry to a 30 cm/12 inch circle and put it on a prepared baking sheet. Brush the pastry with beaten egg. Spoon the ricotta mixture into the centre of the pastry, leaving a 7 cm/3 inch border around the sides. Place the roasted vegetables and chorizo on top of the ricotta mixture.

Fold in the pastry border so that it partly overlaps the filling. Brush the sides with more beaten egg. Scatter with rosemary sprigs and season to taste with salt and pepper. Bake in a preheated oven for 30–35 minutes until the pastry is golden.

Pork and Cider Pie

Serves 4–6

1 tablespoon plain flour
2 teaspoons paprika
750 g/1½ lb lean pork, such as fillet, cubed
2 tablespoons oil
1 onion, chopped
450 ml/¾ pint dry cider
2 teaspoons wholegrain mustard
2 eating apples, peeled, cored and sliced
3 tablespoons thick Greek yogurt
salt and pepper

Pastry
75 g/3 oz butter
6 spring onions, chopped
175 g/6 oz plain flour
125 g/4 oz mashed potato
milk, to glaze
1 teaspoon mustard seeds

Combine the flour, paprika and seasoning in a polythene bag. Add the pork and toss well. Heat the oil in a large frying pan, add the onion and fry for 5 minutes, until softened. Add the pork and fry until lightly browned. Stir in any leftover flour and cook for 1 minute. Stir in the cider, cooking until the mixture is thick. Stir in the mustard, add the apple slices and bring to the boil. Lower the heat, cover and simmer for 40 minutes, until the pork is tender, then leave to cool.

Melt 25 g/1 oz of the butter in a small pan, add the spring onions and fry until softened. Cool slightly. Put the flour in a bowl. Cut the remaining butter into cubes and rub it into the flour until the mixture resembles fine breadcrumbs. Add the spring onions with the cooking juices, then stir in the mashed potato and seasoning.

Stir the yogurt into the pork mixture; turn it into a 1.8 litre/3 pint pie dish. Dampen the rim of the dish with water. Roll out the pastry to a size 5 cm/2 inches larger than the dish and cover the pie. Press the edges to seal, brush with milk and sprinkle with the seeds.

Bake the pie in a preheated oven, 200°C (400°F), Gas Mark 6 for 30 minutes, until the pastry is crisp and golden brown.

Ratatouille Pie

Serves 4–6

2 tablespoons olive oil
1 large onion, sliced thinly
2 garlic cloves, chopped
2 red peppers, cored, seeded and chopped
1 yellow pepper, cored, seeded and chopped
1 large aubergine, chopped
1 x 425 g/14 oz can chopped tomatoes
1 tablespoon tomato purée
1 tablespoon torn basil leaves
3 courgettes, sliced
salt and pepper
beaten egg or milk, to glaze

Pastry
175 g/6 oz plain flour
75 g/3 oz chilled butter, diced
25 g/1 oz grated Parmesan cheese
pinch of chilli powder
1 egg yolk

Heat the oil in a large pan, add the onion and fry for 10 minutes, until softened. Stir in the garlic and peppers and fry for 5 minutes. Stir in the aubergine, tomatoes and tomato purée with salt and pepper to taste. Bring to the boil, lower the heat, cover and simmer for 20 minutes, then add the basil and courgettes and cook for 5 minutes more. Remove from the heat.

Place the flour in a bowl, add the butter and rub in with the fingertips until the mixture resembles fine breadcrumbs. Stir in the Parmesan and chilli powder, then add the egg yolk and enough cold water, about 1–2 tablespoons, to mix to a firm dough. Turn the dough out on a lightly floured surface and knead briefly. Roll out thinly and cut into 2.5 cm/1 inch wide strips.

Turn the filling into a 1.2 litre/2 pint pie dish. Brush the rim of the dish with water and place a pastry strip all round, moisten with water. Arrange the pastry strips decoratively over the pie. Brush with egg or milk. Bake in a preheated oven, 200°C (400°F), Gas Mark 6 for 35–40 minutes, until the pastry is crisp and golden. Serve hot.

Camembert and Cranberry Pie

Serves 4

75 g/3 oz fresh or frozen cranberries
25 g/1 oz sugar
3 tablespoons water
1 tablespoon port
8 sheets filo pastry
25 g/1 oz butter, melted
1 whole Camembert cheese, about 250 g/8 oz
pepper

Place the cranberries in a small saucepan with the sugar, water and
port. Bring to the boil, then lower the heat and simmer gently until
the cranberries pop and are just tender. This should take about
5 minutes. Leave to cool.

Layer the filo pastry on a greased baking sheet, brushing each
layer with melted butter and arranging each one at a slightly
different angle from the previous sheet to form points all round the
edge. Place the Camembert in the centre and spread the cranberry
sauce over the top. Season with pepper.

Gather up the filo pastry over the cheese and cranberry mixture,
scrunching the edges together. Brush with the remaining butter.

Bake in a preheated oven, 200°C (400°F), Gas Mark 6 for
15–20 minutes, until it is golden. Cool on the baking sheet for
5 minutes, then cut into wedges to serve.

Chicory and Ham Tart

Serves 4–6

3 small heads chicory
2 tablespoons lemon juice
6 slices parma ham or cooked ham
2 eggs
150 ml/¼ pint single cream
25 g/1 oz grated Parmesan cheese
salt and pepper

Pastry
125 g/4 oz plain flour
50 g/2 oz oatmeal
75 g/3 oz butter, diced

Mix together the flour and oatmeal in a bowl. Add the butter and rub in with the fingertips until the mixture resembles fine breadcrumbs. Add 3–4 tablespoons of cold water and mix to a firm dough. Knead briefly on a lightly floured surface, then roll out and line a 20 cm/ 8 inch flan tin.

Line with crumpled foil and bake in a preheated oven, 200°C (400°F) Gas Mark 6 for 10 minutes. Remove the flan case and reduce the oven temperature to 180°C (350°F), Gas Mark 4.

Add the chicory to a saucepan of boiling water with the lemon juice. Cover and cook for 10 minutes, until the chicory is just tender, then drain well.

Cut each chicory head in half lengthways and wrap each piece in a slice of ham. Arrange in the pastry case radiating from the centre. Beat together the eggs, cream, Parmesan and seasoning then pour into the pastry case. Bake the tart for 25–30 minutes, until the filling is firm and golden brown. Serve warm.

Mushroom Quiche

A traditional quiche contains bacon but this one uses mushrooms for a tasty and moist filling. Serve warm or cold.

Serves 4–6

300 g/10 oz rich shortcrust pastry
25 g/1 oz butter
250 g/8 oz mushrooms, sliced
250 ml/8 fl oz single cream
2 eggs, beaten
grated nutmeg
salt and pepper

Make the pastry (see page 15). Roll it out and line a 20 cm/8 inch tart tin. Chill the pastry case for 30 minutes, then bake blind in a preheated oven, 200°C (400°F), Gas Mark 6 for 15 minutes. Remove the paper and beans or foil and return the pastry case to the oven for a further 10 minutes.

To make the filling, melt the butter over a medium heat in a frying pan, add the mushrooms and fry until tender and cooked through, being sure to cook off any liquid.

Beat the cream and eggs in a bowl with the grated nutmeg and season to taste with salt and pepper. Sprinkle the mushrooms over the case and pour the cream and egg filling over the top.

Put the tart tin on a baking sheet and bake in a preheated oven, 180°C (350°F), Gas Mark 4, for 30–35 minutes until the filling is just set and the pastry is golden brown.

Leek and Ham Pie

This filling and comforting supper pie has a deep cheese scone
topping, perfect for a cold winter's night.

Serves 4–6

50 g/2 oz butter
3 leeks, trimmed and sliced
40 g/1½ oz plain flour
300 ml/½ pint milk
150 ml/¼ pint vegetable stock
175 g/6 oz thickly sliced cooked ham, chopped
salt and pepper

Scone crust
250 g/8 oz self-raising flour
50 g/2 oz chilled butter, diced
75 g/3 oz mature Cheddar cheese, grated
6–8 tablespoons milk, plus extra to glaze

Melt the butter in a saucepan, add the leeks and fry gently until
softened. Stir in the flour and cook for 1 minute. Gradually add the
milk and vegetable stock, stirring until the sauce is thickened and
smooth. Lower the heat and simmer for 5 minutes, then remove from
the heat and stir in the chopped ham with salt and pepper to taste.

To make the scone crust, place the flour in a bowl with a little salt
and pepper. Add the butter and rub in until the mixture resembles
fine breadcrumbs. Stir in the cheese, then add the milk and mix
quickly to a soft dough.

Turn the leek mixture into a greased 1.2 litre/2 pint ovenproof
dish. Press out the scone crust on a lightly floured surface to the
same size as the dish. Cut into 8 wedges, then place on top of the pie
to cover the dish. Brush with milk.

Bake the pie in a preheated oven, 200°C (400°F), Gas Mark 6, for
25–30 minutes until the top is golden brown. Serve hot.

Steak and Kidney Pie

Serves 6

750 g / 1 ½ lb braising steak, cubed
250 g / 8 oz ox kidney, cored and trimmed
1 large onion, chopped
1 celery stick, chopped
2 carrots, chopped
300 ml / ½ pint water
½ teaspoon dried thyme
1 tablespoon soy sauce
1 tablespoon cornflour
2 tablespoons chopped fresh parsley
375 g / 12 oz puff pastry, thawed if frozen
salt and pepper
beaten egg, to glaze

Combine the steak, kidney, onion, celery and carrots in a large saucepan. Add the water, thyme and soy sauce with salt and pepper to taste. Bring to the boil, then lower the heat, cover and simmer for about 1 ½ hours, until the meat is tender.

Taste and add more seasoning if necessary. In a cup, blend the cornflour to a paste with a little water. Stir into the pan, cooking until the meat sauce is thickened and smooth. Stir in the parsley and leave to cool.

Roll out half the pastry on a lightly floured surface and line a 1.2 litre / 2 pint ovenproof dish or a 23 cm / 9 inch pie plate. Place the cooled meat mixture over the pastry. Dampen the edges with water. Roll out the remaining pastry and cover the pie. Trim the edges, then cut up the edges with a knife and flute to seal and decorate.

Reroll the pastry trimmings and cut into leaves. Attach to the pie with a little of the beaten egg. Brush the top of the pie with more egg and bake in a preheated oven, 220°C (425°F), Gas Mark 7 for 35–40 minutes, until the pastry is crisp and golden brown. Serve hot.

Chicken Pie

Serves 4-6

1 tablespoon plain flour
4 skinless chicken portions, halved
25 g/1 oz butter
1 tablespoon olive oil
2 onions, chopped
300 ml/½ pint chicken stock
2 tablespoons lemon juice
150 ml/¼ pint double cream
1 bunch of parsley, chopped
salt and pepper

Pastry
250 g/8 oz plain flour
125 g/4 oz chilled butter, diced
milk, to glaze

To make the pastry, place the flour in a bowl, add the butter and rub in with the fingertips until the mixture resembles fine breadcrumbs. Add enough cold water, about 3–4 tablespoons, to mix to a firm dough. Knead on a lightly floured surface, wrap closely and chill.

Put the flour in a stout polythene bag and season. Add the chicken and toss until coated. Melt the butter and oil in a frying pan, add the onions and fry for 5 minutes. Remove and set aside. Add the chicken to the pan and fry for 10 minutes. Transfer to a 1.5 litre/2 ½ pint pie dish. Sprinkle the onions over the top. Stir any remaining flour into the pan and cook for 1 minute. Gradually add the stock, stirring until thick. Stir in the lemon juice, cream and parsley and season to taste. Bring to the boil then pour it over the chicken.

Roll out the pastry to measure 5 cm/2 inches larger than the pie dish. Cut off a 2.5 cm/1 inch strip all round, dampen the dish rim and attach the pastry strip. Brush with water and cover the pie with the remaining pastry. Make a hole in the centre to allow the steam to escape. Brush with milk and bake in a preheated oven, 200°C (400°F), Gas Mark 6 for 30 minutes, then reduce to 180°C (350°F), Gas Mark 4 and bake for a further 45 minutes. Serve hot.

Salmon and Red Pepper Pie

Serves 4–6

2 tablespoons olive oil
2 red peppers, cored, seeded and chopped
2 eggs, boiled, peeled and chopped
250 g/8 oz salmon fillet, skinned and cubed
1 courgette, sliced
1 teaspoon chopped dill

Pastry
375 g/12 oz plain flour
175 g/6 oz chilled butter
2 egg yolks
salt and pepper
beaten egg or milk, to glaze

Heat the oil in a saucepan. Add the peppers, with salt and pepper to taste. Cook gently for about 10 minutes, until softened. Purée in a blender or food processor. Alternatively, press the peppers through a sieve into a mixing bowl. Add the chopped eggs to the pepper purée with the salmon, courgette and dill. Mix well.

To make the pastry, place the flour with ½ teaspoon salt in a bowl. Add the butter and rub it in with the fingertips until the mixture resembles fine breadcrumbs. Add the egg yolks with enough cold water, about 3–4 tablespoons, to mix to a firm dough.

Turn the dough out on a lightly floured surface and knead briefly. Roll out just over half and line a 23 cm/9 inch pie plate. Fill with the salmon mixture and dampen the edges of the pastry with water.

Roll out the remaining pastry and cover the pie. Pinch the edges to seal, then crimp the edges to decorate. Reroll the pastry trimmings and cut them into fish tails or leaf shapes to decorate the pie. Attach the shapes with a little of the beaten egg or milk, then brush more egg or milk over the pie to glaze.

Bake the pie in a preheated oven, 200°C (400°F), Gas Mark 6 for 35–40 minutes, until the pastry is crisp and golden brown. Serve hot.

Empanadas

Makes 12

2 spring onions, chopped
1 tomato, chopped
50 g/2 oz cooked ham, chopped
50 g/2 oz Cheddar cheese, grated
1 x 200 g/7 oz can creamed sweetcorn
1 teaspoon chilli sauce
salt and pepper
oil, for deep frying

Pastry
250 g/8 oz plain flour
1 teaspoon paprika
50 g/2 oz butter
1 tablespoon olive oil
125 ml/4 fl oz water

Mix the flour and paprika with ½ teaspoon of salt in a bowl. Heat the butter, oil and water in a pan until the butter has melted. Stir the mixture into the flour and mix to a soft dough. Turn out on to a lightly floured surface and knead briefly. Wrap closely and leave to rest at room temperature for 30 minutes.

Place all the filling ingredients in a bowl and mix well. Roll out the pastry thinly on a lightly floured surface. Cut into twelve 10 cm/4 inch rounds using a pastry cutter. Place 2 teaspoons of filling on each round. Brush the pastry edges with water and fold each round in half. Pinch the edges to seal and decorate.

Pour oil to a depth of about 2.5 cm/1 inch into a large frying pan. Heal the oil and fry the empanadas, a few at a time, for about 5 minutes, turning once, until evenly browned. Remove from the hot oil with a slotted spoon and drain on paper towels. Serve hot.

Crusty Shepherd's Pie

Instead of the traditional mashed potato, this shepherd's pie has a
cheese scone topping.

Serves 4–6

1 tablespoon olive oil
4 rindless smoked streaky bacon rashers, chopped
1 onion, chopped
500 g/1 lb minced lamb
1 teaspoon dried oregano
2 tablespoons chopped fresh parsley
150 ml/¼ pint red wine
425 g/14 oz canned or bottled passata
salt and pepper

Scone topping
250 g/8 oz self-raising flour
50 g/2 oz chilled butter, diced
2 teaspoons wholegrain mustard
75 g/3 oz mature Cheddar cheese, grated
125 ml/4 fl oz milk

Heat the oil in a frying pan, add the bacon and onion and fry for
5 minutes, until softened. Add the lamb and fry, stirring, until evenly
browned. Stir in the herbs, wine and passata with salt and pepper to
taste. Bring to the boil, lower the heat and simmer, uncovered, for
about 25 minutes, until the lamb is tender and the sauce thickened.

Place the flour in a bowl with salt and pepper. Add the butter and
rub in with the fingertips until the mixture resembles fine
breadcrumbs. Stir in the mustard and 50 g/2 oz of the cheese, then
add enough of the milk to mix to a soft dough.

Knead the dough briefly on a lightly floured surface, then roll out
to a thickness of 1 cm/½ inch. Stamp into 5 cm/2 inch scones. Reroll
the trimmings and stamp out more rounds.

Transfer the meat mixture to a greased 1.2 litre/2 pint pie dish.
Arrange the scones over the top, brush with milk and sprinkle with
the remaining cheese. Bake in a preheated oven, 200°C (400°F), Gas
Mark 6 for 25 minutes, until the topping is golden brown. Serve hot.

Ham and Potato Pie

Serves 4–6

175 g/6 oz plain flour
75 g/3 oz chilled butter, diced
50 g/2 oz mature Cheddar cheese, grated
milk or beaten egg, to glaze

Filling
2 tablespoons oil
1 onion, chopped
175 g/6 oz thickly sliced ham, chopped
50 g/2 oz sun-dried tomatoes, chopped
2 tablespoons chopped fresh parsley
3 tablespoons double cream
750 g/1½ lb floury potatoes, cooked and sliced thinly
salt and pepper

Place the flour in a large bowl, add the diced butter and rub in with
the fingertips until the mixture resembles fine breadcrumbs. Stir in
the grated cheese with a little salt and pepper, then add enough cold
water, about 2–3 tablespoons, to make a firm dough.

Knead the dough briefly on a lightly floured surface, wrap closely
and leave to rest while you prepare the filling.

Heat the oil in a frying pan, add the chopped onion and fry for
about 5 minutes, until softened. Add the ham, sun-dried tomatoes,
parsley and cream, with salt and pepper to taste. Bring to the boil,
stirring until heated through.

Layer half the potatoes in a 1.5 litre/2½ pint pie dish and spread
the ham mixture on top. Cover with the remaining potatoes. Roll out
the pastry to measure 5 cm/2 inches larger than the pie dish. Cut off
a 2.5cm/1 inch strip all round and stick this to the rim of the pie dish
with a little water. Moisten the pastry strip with water, then cover
the pie with the remaining pastry, pressing the edges to seal. Make a
hole in the centre of the pie to allow the steam to escape. Brush the
pastry with milk or egg and bake in a preheated oven, 200°C (400°F),
Gas Mark 6 for 35 minutes, until the pastry is crisp and golden
brown. Serve hot.

Scalloped Fish Pie

Instead of pastry, this flavoursome fish pie is topped with sliced potatoes which become golden and crisp in the oven.

Serves 4

750 g/1½ lb haddock or cod fillet
2 bay leaves
6 peppercorns
450 ml/¾ pint milk
65 g/2½ oz butter
1 leek, trimmed, cleaned and sliced
40 g/1½ oz plain flour
2 tomatoes, skinned and quartered
2 tablespoons chopped fresh parsley
750 g/1½ lb potatoes, cooked and sliced thinly
salt and pepper

Place the fish in a frying pan with the bay leaves, peppercorns and milk. Add a little salt and pepper. Bring to the boil then cover, lower the heat and simmer for about 10 minutes, until the fish is tender and flakes easily when tested with the tip of a knife. Using a slotted spoon, remove the fish from the pan; remove the skin and flake the flesh. Strain the cooking liquid into a jug.

Melt 40 g/1½ oz of the butter in a saucepan, add the sliced leek and fry for about 5 minutes until softened. Stir in the plain flour and cook for 1 minute. Gradually add the milk, stirring until the sauce is thickened and smooth.

Remove the pan from the heat and stir in the fish, tomatoes and parsley with salt and pepper to taste. Melt the remaining butter in a small saucepan. Turn the fish mixture into a greased 1.2 litre/2 pint ovenproof dish. Arrange the potatoes over the top in overlapping rows. Brush with the butter. Bake the pie in a preheated oven, 200°C (400°F), Gas Mark 6 for 25 minutes, until the topping is golden brown. Serve hot with mange tout.

Spiced Lentil Pie

Serves 6

2 tablespoons sunflower oil
2 cloves garlic, crushed
1 onion, chopped
2 sticks celery, chopped
1 red pepper, seeded and chopped
125 g/4 oz red lentils
3 ripe tomatoes, skinned and chopped
$^3/_4$ teaspoon chilli powder
450 ml/$^3/_4$ pint vegetable stock
3 tablespoons chopped fresh coriander
2 tablespoons lemon juice
salt and pepper
beaten egg, to glaze

Pastry
375 g/12 oz plain flour
175 g/6 oz butter or margarine, diced
2 teaspoons cumin seeds
2 teaspoons ground coriander
$^1/_2$ teaspoon chilli powder
3 tablespoons lemon juice

Place the flour in a bowl. Add the butter and rub in with the fingertips until the mixture resembles breadcrumbs. Stir in the spices and salt, then add the lemon juice and 1–2 tablespoons of water and mix to a firm dough. Wrap closely and leave to rest.

Heat the oil, add the garlic and onion and fry for 5 minutes. Add the celery and red pepper and cook for a further 2 minutes. Stir in the lentils, tomatoes, chilli powder and stock and simmer uncovered for 25–30 minutes, until the lentils have absorbed the stock. Season, then stir in the coriander and lemon juice. Leave to cool.

Roll out just over half the pastry and line a 23 cm/9 inch pie plate. Spread over the filling and brush the pastry edges with water.

Roll out the remaining pastry and cover the pie. Pinch the edges together to seal. Brush the top with egg and bake in a preheated oven 200°C (400°F), Gas Mark 6 for 35–40 minutes, until golden brown. Cover with foil if it starts to over brown. Serve hot with a salad.

Turkey, Spinach and Brie Filo Pie

Serves 6–8

175 g/6 oz frozen leaf spinach, thawed
75 g/3 oz butter
1 tablespoon olive oil
25 g/1 oz pine nuts
375 g/12 oz boneless turkey breast, cut into strips
175 g/6 oz Brie cheese, rind removed, cut into chunks
4 spring onions, chopped
1 teaspoon dried oregano
grated rind and juice of 1 lemon
250 g/8 oz frozen filo pastry, thawed
salt and pepper

Put the spinach in a colander. Press out the excess water, then chop roughly. Melt 25 g/1 oz of the butter with the oil in a pan. Add the pine nuts and brown. Add the turkey and fry until browned, lower the heat and fry for 5 minutes, until cooked. Transfer the contents of the pan to a bowl. Stir in the spinach, Brie, onions, oregano, lemon rind and juice. Season to taste and mix.

Grease a baking sheet and have the filo pastry ready, keeping the sheets of pastry covered while you work. Melt the remaining butter in a small pan.

Place 3 sheets of filo down the length of the baking sheet, overlapping each sheet by 2.5 cm/1 inch and brushing each with the melted butter (the pastry will overlap the baking sheet). Continue layering the sheets until you have 3 layers of pastry, brushing each layer with butter. Put the spinach filling on the centre third of the pastry to within 2.5 cm/1 inch of the top and bottom edges. Layer the remaining pastry sheets over the filling, brushing each with butter. Draw the top and bottom filo edges over, fold in both sides to enclose the filling, then scrunch the pastry on top.

Bake in a preheated oven, 200°C (400°F), Gas Mark 6 for 25 minutes, until the pastry is golden and crisp. Serve warm.

Three Cheese Puff Pie

This rich, tasty pie is full of wonderful melted cheese and very simple to make. Serve with a crisp green salad.

Serves 4–6

125 g/4 oz mozzarella cheese
175 g/6 oz Gorgonzola cheese
25 g/1 oz grated Parmesan cheese
25 g/1 oz pecan nuts, chopped
4 spring onions, chopped finely
2 tablespoons chopped fresh parsley
3 tablespoons crème fraîche
pepper
375 g/12 oz puff pastry, thawed if frozen
beaten egg, to glaze

Chop the mozzarella and Gorgonzola into pieces. Reserve 2 teaspoons of the Parmesan and mix the remainder with the other cheeses in a bowl. Add the pecans, spring onions, parsley and crème fraîche with pepper to taste. Mix well.

Roll out half the pastry on a lightly floured surface to a 23 cm/ 9 inch square. Place on a greased baking sheet. Spread the cheese mixture over the top to within 1 cm/½ inch of the edges. Roll out the remaining pastry to a slightly larger square. Dampen the edges of the pastry with water and cover the pie. Press the edges together to seal and trim the edges if necessary. Flute the edge of the pie with the back of a sharp knife to form scallops.

Brush the top with the egg and sprinkle with the reserved Parmesan. Bake the pie in a preheated oven, 200°C (400°F), Gas Mark 6 for 25 minutes, until the pastry is golden. Serve hot.

Treacle Tart

This old nursery stand-by is hard to beat on a cold winter's day, or indeed on any other day. Serve it with plenty of custard or cream.

Serves 6

300 g/ 10 oz shortcrust pastry
275 g/ 9 oz golden syrup
175 g/ 6 oz fresh white breadcrumbs
grated rind and juice of 2 lemons

Roll out the pastry and use to line a deep 20 cm/8 inch tart tin. Trim the edges. Warm the golden syrup in a saucepan until it is runny, then remove the pan from the heat and stir in the breadcrumbs, lemon rind and juice. Spread the mixture over the pastry case.

Bake the tart in a preheated oven, 200°C (400°F), Gas Mark 6 for 30–35 minutes until the pastry is crisp and the filling golden. Serve warm or cold, drizzled with extra golden syrup.

Orange and Walnut Pie

Serves 8–10

125 g/4 oz dark muscovado sugar
4 tablespoons molasses
4 tablespoons golden syrup
75 g/3 oz butter, melted
1 teaspoon vanilla essence
grated rind of 1 orange
4 eggs, beaten
175 g/6 oz walnut halves

Pastry
250 g/8 oz plain flour
125 g/4 oz chilled butter, diced
25 g/1 oz caster sugar

To make the pastry, place the flour in a bowl. Add the butter and rub in with the fingertips until the mixture resembles fine breadcrumbs. Stir in the sugar, then add enough cold water, about 3–4 tablespoons, to mix to a firm dough.

Turn the dough out on to a lightly floured surface and knead briefly. Roll out the dough and use to line a 28 x 18 cm/11 x 7 inch shallow oblong tin. Chill the pastry case for 30 minutes.

To make the filling, mix the sugar, molasses, syrup, butter and vanilla in a bowl. Stir in the orange rind and eggs and mix well. Chop half the nuts and add to the filling mixture. Pour into the prepared pastry case.

Arrange the remaining walnut halves over the top of the pie. Bake in a preheated oven, 180°C (350°F), Gas Mark 4 for 45–50 minutes until the pastry is golden brown and the filling has set. Leave to cool, then cut into squares and serve.

Baked Custard Tart

Fresh nutmeg has a far superior flavour to the ready grated spice. Keep nutmegs in an airtight container so that the aroma and flavour are not dissipated.

Serves 6

300 g/10 oz shortcrust pastry
4 eggs
25 g/1 oz caster sugar
½ teaspoon vanilla essence
450 ml/¾ pint milk
grated nutmeg

Roll out the pastry and line a 20 cm/8 inch tart tin. Chill for 30 minutes, then bake blind in a preheated oven, 200°C (400°F), Gas Mark 6 for 15 minutes. Remove the paper and beans or foil and return to the oven for a further 5 minutes.

Lightly whisk the eggs with the sugar and vanilla essence in a bowl. Heat the milk until warm and whisk into the egg mixture.

Strain the custard into the pastry case and sprinkle with grated nutmeg. Bake in a preheated oven, 160°C (325°F), Gas Mark 3, for 45–50 minutes until the custard is set and lightly browned. Serve warm or cold.

Royal Curd Tart

This is a rich, filling tart, so use unsweetened pastry for the case.
Curd cheese gives the filling a creamy smoothness that is not over
sweet. Fresh strawberries are a good accompaniment.

Serves 6

375 g / 12 oz shortcrust pastry
225 g / 7½ oz medium-fat curd cheese
50 g / 2 oz ground almonds
50 g / 2 oz caster sugar
2 eggs, separated
grated rind and juice of 1 lemon
50 g / 2 oz sultanas
150 ml / ¼ pint double cream
icing sugar, to decorate

Roll out the pastry and use it to line a 23 cm/9 inch flan ring placed
on a baking sheet. Prick the base, then chill for 30 minutes.

Put the curd cheese into a bowl and blend in the ground almonds,
caster sugar and egg yolks. Add the lemon rind and juice, sultanas
and cream and mix.

Whisk the egg whites until stiff and fold them into the mixture.
Pour the mixture into the pastry case and bake in a preheated oven,
200°C (400°F), Gas Mark 6 for 20 minutes. Lower the temperature to
180°C (350°F), Gas Mark 4 and cook for a further 30–35 minutes
until firm and golden. Dust the tart with icing sugar and serve
warm or chilled.

Pumpkin Pie

To make pumpkin purée, steam or boil pumpkin chunks for
15–20 minutes until tender, then drain thoroughly. Purée the pieces
in a food processor or blender, or press them through a sieve.

Serves 6–8

375 g/12 oz pâte sucrée
250 g/8 oz pumpkin purée
2 eggs, beaten
150 ml/¼ pint single cream
75 g/3 oz caster sugar
1 teaspoon ground cinnamon, plus extra for sprinkling
½ teaspoon ground ginger
¼ teaspoon grated nutmeg
150 ml/¼ pint whipping cream

Make the pastry (see page 16). Roll it out and line a 23 cm/9 inch pie
dish. Gather up the trimmings, reroll them thinly and cut into leaf
shapes. Brush the edge of the pie lightly with water and attach the
leaves around the rim.

Mix the pumpkin purée, eggs, cream, sugar and spices in a bowl.
Pour into the pastry case. Bake the pie in a preheated oven, 200°C
(400°F), Gas Mark 6 for 45–50 minutes until the filling has set.
Leave to cool.

Whip the cream in a bowl until stiff. Spoon cream swirls around
the rim of the pie and sprinkle with a little ground cinnamon.

Blueberry Shortcake Tart

Serves 6

250 g/8 oz fresh or frozen blueberries
25 g/1 oz sugar
milk, for brushing
50 g/2 oz flaked almonds

Pastry
375 g/12 oz self-raising flour
175 g/6 oz chilled butter, diced
125 g/4 oz caster sugar
1 egg, beaten

Place the flour in a bowl, add the butter and rub it in until the mixture resembles fine breadcrumbs. Stir in the caster sugar. Add the egg and mix to a firm dough, adding a little cold water, if necessary.

Roll out two-thirds of the pastry and use to line a greased 23 cm/9 inch tart tin. Spread the blueberries evenly over the pastry case and sprinkle with the sugar.

Roll out the remaining pastry and cut into thin strips. Brush the rim of the tart with water and arrange the pastry strips in a lattice pattern over the top. Brush the pastry with a little milk and sprinkle with the flaked almonds.

Bake in a preheated oven, 190°C (375°F), Gas Mark 5 for 30–35 minutes, until the pastry is golden and the blueberries are tender. Serve the tart warm or cold with cream or crème fraîche.

Pear and Almond Tart

This is the classic French tart – a crisp pastry case filled with moist almond sponge, with pear wedges nestling in it.

Serves 4

50 g/2 oz butter
50 g/2 oz caster sugar
50 g/2 oz ground almonds
few drops almond essence
1 egg, beaten
2 ripe pears, quartered and sliced
2 tablespoons clear honey

Pastry
175 g/6 oz plain flour
75 g/3 oz chilled butter, diced

Place the flour in a bowl, add the butter and rub in with the fingertips until the mixture resembles fine breadcrumbs. Stir in 3–4 tablespoons cold water and mix to a firm dough. Turn the dough out on to a lightly floured surface and knead briefly. Roll out and line a 20 cm/8 inch flan tin.

Beat together the butter and sugar for about 5 minutes, until light and fluffy. Beat in the almonds, almond essence and egg and mix well. Spread over the pastry case.

Arrange the pears over the filling in a haphazard way, pressing them gently into the filling. Bake in a preheated oven, 180°C (350°F), Gas Mark 4 for 35–40 minutes, until the pastry is cooked and golden brown. Warm the honey and brush over the tart. Serve warm or cold.

Alaska Crumble Pie

Serves 4–6

175 g/6 oz oat biscuits
75 g/3 oz butter
3 egg whites
175 g/6 oz caster sugar
125 g/4 oz raspberries
125 g/4 oz redcurrants
500 ml/17 fl oz vanilla ice cream

Crumb the biscuits in a food processor. Alternatively, place them between 2 sheets of greaseproof paper and crush with a rolling pin. Melt the butter in a pan, add the crumbs and stir well. Press the mixture evenly over the base and sides of a 23 cm/9 inch pie plate or flan tin and chill until ready to serve.

Whisk the egg whites in a grease-free bowl until stiff and dry. Whisk in 1 tablespoon of the sugar, then fold in the remainder.

When ready to serve, fill the crumb case with fruit and add scoops of ice cream. Spread the meringue over the top, covering the filling completely. Bake in a preheated oven, 200°C (400°F), Gas Mark 6 for 5–8 minutes, until golden. Serve immediately.

Peach and Honey Pie

Serves 6

6 ripe peaches, stoned and sliced
2 tablespoons clear honey
25 g/1 oz shelled hazelnuts
3 cardamom pods
beaten egg or milk, to glaze
sugar, for sprinkling

Pastry
250 g/8 oz plain flour
125 g/4 oz chilled butter, diced
50 g/2 oz ground hazelnuts
25 g/1 oz caster sugar

Place the flour in a bowl. Add the butter and rub in with the fingertips until the mixture resembles fine breadcrumbs. Stir in the hazelnuts and sugar, then add enough cold water, about 3–4 tablespoons, to mix to a firm dough.

Turn the dough out on to a lightly floured surface and knead briefly. Roll out two-thirds of the dough and line a 23 cm/9 inch pie plate. Wrap the remaining dough closely and set it aside.

Pile the peaches into the pastry case. Drizzle over the honey and sprinkle with the hazelnuts. Split the cardamom pods and scrape out the seeds. Sprinkle the seeds over the filling.

Roll out the remaining dough and cut into 2.5 cm/1 inch wide strips. Brush the edge of the pie with water. Arrange the strips in a lattice design over the pie, with a little of the filling showing.

Brush the pastry with egg or milk and sprinkle with sugar. Bake in a preheated oven, 200°C (400°F), Gas Mark 6 for 35–40 minutes, until the pastry is golden brown. Serve warm or cold.

Autumn Fruit Cobbler

Plums, pears and blackberries – the flavours of autumn – are packed into a dish and finished with a cobbler topping. Serve hot with lashings of cream or custard.

Serves 6–8

500 g/1 lb plums, halved
2 pears, chopped
250 g/8 oz blackberries
50 g/2 oz light muscovado sugar
milk, for brushing
poppy seeds, for sprinkling

Cobbler
250 g/8 oz self-raising flour
50 g/2 oz caster sugar
50 g/2 oz butter, diced
7–8 tablespoons milk

Mix all the fruit together in a bowl and turn into a buttered 1.2 litre/ 2 pint ovenproof dish. Mix together the flour and sugar. Add the butter and rub in with the fingertips until the mixture resembles fine breadcrumbs. Stir in the milk and mix to a soft dough.

Roll out the dough to a 20 cm/8 inch square. Cut into 3 each way to make 9 squares. Arrange these over the fruit, brush with milk and sprinkle with poppy seeds.

Bake the cobbler in a preheated oven, 200°C (400°F), Gas Mark 6 for about 25–30 minutes, until the topping is golden brown. Serve hot with cream or custard.

Pear and Blueberry Pie

This is a rough-and-ready pie in which the pastry does not quite
cover the filling on top, giving a rustic charm.

Serves 6–8

4 firm pears, peeled, cored and chopped
500 g/1 lb blueberries
25 g/1 oz butter
50 g/2 oz light muscovado sugar
1 egg white, lightly beaten, to glaze
caster sugar, for dredging

Pastry
250 g/8 oz plain flour
125 g/4 oz chilled butter, diced
25 g/1 oz caster sugar
1 egg yolk

Make the pastry. Place the flour in a bowl, add the butter and rub in
with the fingertips until the mixture resembles fine breadcrumbs. Stir
in the sugar, then add the egg yolk and enough cold water, about
3–4 tablespoons, to mix to a firm dough.

Turn the dough out on to a lightly floured surface and knead
briefly. Roll out to a rough round about 35 cm/14 inches across. Lift
the round on to a 23 cm/9 inch pie plate. Fill the centre of the pie
with the pears and blueberries, dot with the butter and sprinkle with
the muscovado sugar. Fold the overlapping pastry over the filling.
Some of the filling will still show.

Brush the top of the pastry with egg white and dredge with
caster sugar. Bake in a preheated oven, 200°C (400°F), Gas Mark 6
for 35–40 minutes until the pastry is golden brown. Serve warm.

Pecan Pie

This classic pie has a rich toffee-like mixture spread over a crisp pastry base, and is topped with crunchy pecan nuts.

Serves 8–10

125 g/4 oz dark muscovado sugar
4 tablespoons molasses
4 tablespoons golden syrup
75 g/3 oz butter, melted
1 teaspoon vanilla essence
grated rind of 1 lemon
4 eggs, beaten
175 g/6 oz pecan halves

Pastry
250 g/8 oz plain flour
125 g/4 oz chilled butter, diced
25 g/1 oz caster sugar

Place the flour in a bowl. Add the butter and rub in with the fingertips until the mixture resembles fine breadcrumbs. Stir in the sugar, then add enough cold water, about 3–4 tablespoons, to mix to a firm dough.

Turn the dough out on to a lightly floured surface and knead briefly. Roll out the dough and use to line a 28 x 18 cm/11 x 7 inch shallow oblong tin. Chill the pastry case for 30 minutes.

To make the filling, mix the sugar, molasses, syrup, butter and vanilla in a bowl. Stir in the lemon rind and eggs and mix well. Chop half the nuts and add to the filling mixture. Pour into the prepared pastry case.

Arrange the remaining pecans over the top of the pie. Bake in a preheated oven, 180°C (350°F), Gas Mark 4 for 45–50 minutes until the pastry is golden brown and the filling has set. Leave to cool, then cut into squares and serve.

Special Treats

Pies and tarts can be glamorous as well as everyday. The following selection offers a mouth-watering array of flavours, perfect for a special occasion – perhaps a formal dinner or birthday meal – but also tempting as an indulgent weekend treat for the family.

Dolcelatte and Leek Galette

Creamy blue dolcelatte has a smooth, mild flavour, which is ideal in rich sauces. Do not overcook the leeks as they will become tough and unpalatable.

Serves 4

8 thin leeks
300 g/10 oz puff pastry, defrosted if frozen
50 ml/2 fl oz crème fraîche
1 teaspoon cayenne pepper
1 tablespoon wholegrain mustard
50 g/2 oz dolcelatte cheese, crumbled
1 egg, beaten
salt and pepper
chopped parsley, to garnish (optional)

Trim the leeks to 20 cm/8 inches and put them in a frying pan. Pour in enough boiling water to cover them and bring back to the boil. Reduce the heat, cover the pan and simmer for 5–7 minutes. Drain the leeks and set aside.

Roll out the pastry to about 25 cm/10 inches square and put it on a prepared baking sheet. Use a sharp knife to score all the way round the pastry 3.5 cm/1½ inches in from the edge; do not cut right through the pastry.

Pat the leeks dry with kitchen paper to remove any excess moisture and arrange them on the pastry inside the border.

Mix together the crème fraîche, cayenne, mustard and cheese and gently spread the mixture over the leeks. Season well with salt and pepper and cook in a preheated oven, 220°C (425°F), Gas Mark 7 for 15 minutes or until the pastry has risen and the border has browned. Cut the galette into quarters and sprinkle each portion with chopped parsley, if using. Serve immediately.

Asparagus, Parmesan and Egg Tart

This tart makes good use of a small amount of asparagus. Use young, thin spears and cut off the thick, woody section at the base.

Serves 4

375 g/12 oz shortcrust pastry
175 g/6 oz thin asparagus spears
5 eggs
150 ml/¼ pint single cream
25 g/1 oz grated Parmesan cheese
salt and pepper

Roll out the pastry and line a 20 cm/8 inch tart tin. Chill the pastry case for 30 minutes, then bake blind in a preheated oven, 200°C (400°F), Gas Mark 6 for 15 minutes. Remove the paper and beans or foil and return the tart to the oven for a further 10 minutes.

Meanwhile, trim the woody ends from the asparagus. Stand the spears upright in a tall saucepan and add salted boiling water to cover all but the tips of the asparagus. Cover the pan and cook for 7–10 minutes, until tender. Drain the asparagus in a colander and refresh under cold running water. Drain again.

Beat one of the eggs in a bowl with the cream and season to taste with salt and pepper. Arrange the asparagus in the base of the pastry case. Break each of the remaining eggs in turn into a saucer and carefully slide them into the pastry case.

Pour the cream mixture over the eggs, sprinkle with Parmesan and bake the tart in a preheated oven, 180°C (350°F), Gas Mark 4, for 15–20 minutes until the eggs have just set. Serve warm.

Gorgonzola and Hazelnut Quiche

Serves 6–8

50 g/2 oz butter
1 tablespoon vegetable oil
2 large leeks, thinly sliced
150 ml/¼ pint whipping cream
150 ml/¼ pint milk
2 tablespoons chopped flat-leaf parsley
2 eggs, beaten
125 g/4 oz Gorgonzola cheese, crumbled
75 g/3 oz whole hazelnuts, lightly toasted
salt and pepper

Pastry
250 g/8 oz plain flour
pinch of salt
pinch of cayenne pepper
75 g/3 oz chilled butter, diced
25 g/1 oz Cheddar cheese, finely grated
6–8 tablespoons cold water

Make the pastry. Put the flour, salt and cayenne in a bowl, add the butter and rub in with your fingertips until the mixture resembles breadcrumbs. Mix in the grated Cheddar. Add enough water to make a soft, pliable pastry, wrap it in clingfilm and chill for 30 minutes.

Roll out the pastry and line a deep 20 cm/8 inch tart tin. Chill the pastry case for 30 minutes and bake blind in a preheated oven, 190°C (375°F), Gas Mark 5 for 12 minutes. Remove the paper and beans or foil and return to the oven for a further 5 minutes.

Heat the butter and oil in a frying pan and fry the sliced leeks until they are softened and caramelized. Remove from the heat and allow to cool. Beat together the cream, milk, parsley and eggs. Stir the egg mixture into the leeks and season well with salt and pepper. Stir the Gorgonzola into the mixture, then pour it into the pastry case. Smooth the surface, then scatter the hazelnuts over the top.

Bake the quiche in a preheated oven for 40–50 minutes or until the egg mixture has just set in the middle. Remove from the oven and allow to cool slightly before serving with a mixed salad.

Shallot Tarte Tatin

Shallots are related to onions but form a cluster of small bulbs rather than a single one. They have a subtler flavour than onions and are not as pungent as garlic.

Serves 4–6

500 g/1 lb shallots, peeled
25 g/1 oz butter
2 tablespoons olive oil
2 teaspoons muscovado sugar
salt and pepper

Pastry
175 g/6 oz self-raising wholemeal flour
75 g/3 oz chilled butter, diced
2 tablespoons chopped parsley
2 teaspoons chopped thyme
2–3 tablespoons lemon juice

Sift the flour into a bowl and rub in the butter until the mixture resembles breadcrumbs. Stir in the herbs and lemon juice and mix to a firm dough. Knead briefly, then chill for 30 minutes.

Make the filling. Boil the shallots for 10 minutes and drain well. Heat the butter and oil in an ovenproof frying pan, and gently fry the shallots, stirring, for about 10 minutes until they start to colour. Sprinkle over the sugar, season to taste with salt and pepper and cook gently for 5 minutes until well coloured.

Roll out the dough to a round, a little larger than the pan. Support the dough on the rolling pin and lay it over the shallots, tucking the edges of the pastry down the side of the pan.

Bake the tart in a preheated oven, 200°C (400°F), Gas Mark 6 for 20–25 minutes until the pastry is crisp. Leave the tart to cool for 5 minutes, then put a large plate over the pan and invert the tart on to it. Serve warm or cold.

Root Vegetable Tatin

Serves 6

3 tablespoons olive oil
175 g/6 oz carrots, cut into 2.5 cm/1 inch chunks
175 g/6 oz turnips, cut into 2.5 cm/1 inch chunks
175 g/6 oz parsnips, cut into 2.5 cm/1 inch chunks
175 g/6 oz shallots, halved if large
1 teaspoon coriander seeds, finely ground
1 teaspoon fennel seeds, finely ground
4 garlic cloves, peeled
175 g/6 oz leeks, cut into 2.5 cm/1 inch chunks
375 g/12 oz puff pastry, defrosted if frozen

Caramel
20 g/¾ oz butter
40 g/1½ oz sugar
1 tablespoon red wine vinegar
25 ml/1 fl oz water

Heat the oil in a roasting tin and add the vegetables and spices. Toss over a high heat until lightly coloured, then transfer to a preheated oven for 20 minutes. Add the garlic and cook for 10 minutes. Add the leeks and cook for a further 10 minutes or until the vegetables are tender and a rich brown colour. Roll out the pastry and cut it into six 12 cm/5 inch circles. Cover and chill until required.

Combine all the ingredients for the caramel in a frying pan, bring to the boil, shaking the pan and stirring until the sugar dissolves, and let the mixture bubble until it turns a deep golden caramel. Keep shaking the pan and drawing a spoon across the centre to disperse the heat. Quickly pour the caramel into the centre of six shallow 7 cm/3 inch heavy pie tins, spreading it over their bases if you can.

Arrange the vegetables over the caramel. Put the pastry discs over them, tucking in the edges. Set the pies on a baking sheet and bake in a preheated oven, 220°C (425°F), Gas Mark 7 for 10–15 minutes until the pastry is golden. Cool for a few minutes, then invert on to warmed plates, handling the tarts carefully as the hot juices may run out. Serve the tarts hot, pastry side down.

Onion, Raisin and Pine Nut Tart

The slightly resinous, spicy flavour of pine nuts combines perfectly with the mozzarella in this simple tart, which makes a delicious lunchtime treat.

Serves 4

75 g/3 oz butter
2 teaspoons mustard seeds
150 g/5 oz plain flour
125 g/4 oz mashed potato
2 tablespoons olive oil
2 onions, thinly sliced
125 g/4 oz mozzarella cheese, sliced
25 g/1 oz pine nuts
25 g/1 oz raisins
salt and pepper

Heat 25 g/1 oz of the butter in a frying pan and fry the mustard seeds until they start to pop. Cut the remaining butter into cubes and rub it into the flour in a bowl. Stir in the mashed potato and the mustard seeds with the melted butter. Season to taste with salt and pepper and mix to a soft dough.

Press the dough out to form a 25 cm/10 inch square and put it on a prepared baking sheet. Neatly pinch the edges to make a rim.

Heat the oil in a frying pan, add the onions and fry for about 5 minutes until soft and lightly browned. Arrange the mozzarella slices evenly over the pastry base, then scatter the pine nuts and raisins over the top. Cover with the onions and sprinkle with salt and pepper. Bake the tart in a preheated oven, 200°C (400°F), Gas Mark 6 for 25–30 minutes until the pastry is golden brown. Serve hot.

Butternut Squash and Jarlsberg Tart with Oregano Oil

Jarlsberg is a soft Norwegian cheese with a slightly nutty flavour.
If you cannot find Jarlsberg, use Emmenthal instead.

Serves 6

375 g/12 oz shortcrust pastry
1 tablespoon sun-dried tomato paste
1 kg/2 lb butternut squash, peeled, halved and sliced
(about 625 g/1¼ lb) prepared weight
250 g/8 oz Jarlsberg cheese, rind removed and thinly sliced
2 tablespoons chopped oregano
3 tablespoons olive oil
6 thin slices Parma ham

Roll out the pastry and line a 25 cm/10 inch fluted tart tin. Spread
the tomato paste over the base and chill for 30 minutes.

Arrange the slices of butternut in the tart, overlapping each slice
with the next. Push the slices of cheese between the slices of
butternut squash.

Stir the oregano into the oil and use half to brush over the tart.
Bake the tart in a preheated oven, 180°C (350°F), Gas Mark 4 for
30 minutes. Remove from the oven. Loosely arrange the slices of
Parma ham over the tart, brush with the remaining herb oil and
return to the oven for a further 30 minutes. Serve hot.

Smoked Haddock and Spinach Tart

Serves 4–6

350 g/11½ oz smoked haddock fillet
300 ml/½ pint milk
125 g/4 oz frozen leaf spinach, defrosted
40 g/1½ oz butter
25 g/1 oz plain flour
2 eggs, beaten
75 g/3 oz mature Cheddar cheese, grated
salt and pepper

Pastry
75 g/3 oz wholemeal flour
75 g/3 oz plain flour
75 g/3 oz chilled butter, diced
2–3 tablespoons iced water

Mix the flours in a bowl, add the butter and rub in with the fingertips until the mixture resembles breadcrumbs. Stir in enough water to make a firm dough. Knead the dough briefly and chill for 30 minutes. Roll it out and line a deep 20 cm/8 inch tart tin. Bake the pastry case blind in a preheated oven, 200°C (400°F), Gas Mark 6 for 15 minutes.

Put the haddock in a pan and pour over the milk. Bring to the boil, cover, lower the heat and cook gently for about 10 minutes until the haddock flakes easily. Use a slotted spoon to remove the fish from the pan. Strain the cooking liquid into a jug. Skin and flake the fish.

Press the spinach in a sieve to extract as much liquid as possible. Heat the butter in a pan until bubbling, stir in the flour and cook for 1 minute. Gradually stir in the reserved cooking liquid until the sauce is thick and smooth.

Let the sauce cool for 5 minutes, then stir in the spinach, eggs and haddock. Add 50 g/2 oz of the cheese and season to taste with salt and pepper. Stir well and pour into the pastry case. Sprinkle over the remaining cheese and bake in a preheated oven, 190°C (375°F), Gas Mark 5, for about 25 minutes.

Salmon Tart with Wholegrain Mustard and Rocket

Rocket is related to mustard and watercress; the young leaves have a sharp, peppery flavour that is immediately recognizable.

Serves 4

300 g/10 oz salmon fillet or loin, skinned and all bones removed
250 ml/8 fl oz milk
50 g/2 oz rocket, plus extra leaves to garnish
3 eggs, beaten
3 tablespoons wholegrain mustard
5 spring onions, finely chopped

Pastry
225 g/7½ oz plain flour
100 g/3½ oz butter
grated rind of 1 lemon
1 tablespoon cracked black pepper
4 tablespoons iced water

Put the flour, butter, lemon rind and black pepper in a food processor and blitz until the mixture resembles fine breadcrumbs. Add the water and pulse a few times until the mixture comes together. Cover with clingfilm and chill for 1 hour.

Roll out the pastry and line a deep 20 cm/8 inch fluted tart tin. Chill the pastry case for 30 minutes, then bake blind in a preheated oven, 200°C (400°F), Gas Mark 6 for 15 minutes. Remove the paper and beans or foil and return to the oven for a further 5 minutes.

Poach the salmon in the milk for 5 minutes until cooked. Leave to cool slightly. Put the chopped rocket in the base of the pastry case. Remove the salmon from the milk and strain and reserve the cooking liquid. Break the salmon into pieces and arrange over the rocket.

Beat together the eggs, mustard, spring onions and poaching milk and pour over the salmon. Bake in the oven for 25–30 minutes until golden and firm. Garnish with rocket leaves.

Prawn and Courgette Tart

Use a young courgette with a dark green, glossy skin. As they age, the skins of courgettes become duller and the flavour is less intense.

Serves 4–6

375 g/12 oz shortcrust pastry
40 g/1½ oz butter
1 courgette, cut into matchsticks
25 g/1 oz plain flour
300 ml/½ pint hot milk
175 g/6 oz peeled cooked prawns, defrosted if frozen
2 eggs, beaten
75 g/3 oz mature Cheddar cheese, grated
salt and pepper

Roll out the pastry and line a 23 cm/9 inch tart tin. Chill for 30 minutes, then bake the pastry case blind in a preheated oven, 200°C (400°F), Gas Mark 6 for 15 minutes.

Melt the butter in a saucepan, add the courgette matchsticks and cook gently for about 5 minutes until softened. Stir in the flour and cook for 1 minute. Gradually stir in the hot milk, cooking until the sauce is thick and smooth.

Let the sauce cool slightly, then stir in the prawns and eggs with 50 g/2 oz of the grated cheese. Season to taste with salt and pepper. Pour the filling into the pastry case and sprinkle with the remaining grated cheese.

Bake the tart in a preheated oven, 190°C (375°F), Gas Mark 5, for about 25 minutes until the filling is golden brown. Serve warm.

Leek and Mussel Tart

If you prefer to buy raw mussels you will need about 500 g/1 lb.
Scrub them thoroughly and cook in water over a high heat until the
shells open. Discard any that remain shut.

Serves 4–6

375 g/12 oz rich shortcrust pastry
25 g/1 oz butter
2 leeks, trimmed, cleaned and sliced
175 g/6 oz shelled, cooked mussels
3 tablespoons crème fraîche
2 tablespoons dried breadcrumbs
3 tablespoons chopped parsley
1 garlic clove, chopped
2 tablespoons olive oil
salt and pepper

Roll out the pastry and line a 20 cm/8 inch tart tin. Chill the
pastry case for 30 minutes, then bake blind in a preheated oven,
200°C (400°F), Gas Mark 6 for 15 minutes. Remove the paper and
beans or foil and return the tart to the oven for a further 10 minutes.

Melt the butter in a frying pan and cook the leeks for about
5 minutes until softened and tender. Add the mussels and crème
fraîche to the pan. Season to taste with salt and pepper and stir over a
gentle heat until warmed through.

Mix the breadcrumbs, parsley, garlic and oil in a small bowl. Fill
the warm pastry case with the mussel and leek mixture, then sprinkle
the breadcrumb mixture over the top. Place under a preheated
moderate grill until the crumbs are browned and crisp. Serve warm.

Smoked Chicken and Wild Mushroom Tart

Ordinary roast chicken can be used if you prefer, but the combination of wild mushrooms and smoked meat is mouthwateringly good.

Serves 6

375 g/12 oz shortcrust pastry
1–2 tablespoons olive oil
125 g/4 oz mixed wild mushrooms
½ a cooked smoked chicken
100 g/3½ oz sun-blushed tomatoes
100 g/3½ oz Cheddar cheese, grated
3 eggs
300 ml/½ pint double cream
2 tablespoons chopped tarragon

Roll out the pastry and line a 30 x 20 cm/12 x 8 inch fluted tart tin. Chill the pastry case for 30 minutes, then bake blind in a preheated oven, 200°C (400°F), Gas Mark 6 for 15 minutes. Remove the paper and beans or foil and return to the oven for a further 5 minutes.

Heat the oil in a frying pan and cook the mushrooms for 3–4 minutes until they are lightly coloured and cooked.

Remove the chicken meat from the bones and carcass, cutting the larger pieces into bite-sized chunks. Sprinkle the chicken, tomatoes, mushrooms and cheese into the pastry case.

Mix together the eggs, cream and tarragon. Pour over the filling and bake in a preheated oven for 30–35 minutes until golden and set.

Salmon in Puff Pastry

Serves 6–8

1 kg/2 lb salmon, skinned and filleted
25 g/1 oz butter
2 rindless streaky bacon rashers, chopped
125 g/4 oz mushrooms, chopped
125 g/4 oz soft cheese with garlic and herbs
2 tablespoons milk
500 g/1 lb puff pastry, thawed if frozen
beaten egg, to glaze
salt and pepper

Season the salmon fillets on both sides. Melt the butter in a frying pan, add the bacon and fry for about 5 minutes, until crisp. Add the mushrooms and fry for about 2 minutes, until softened, stirring all the time. Stir in the soft cheese and milk with salt and pepper to taste. Cook gently, stirring until well mixed. Remove from the heat and leave to cool.

Roll out half the pastry to measure 2.5 cm/1 inch larger all round than the reassembled fish. Transfer the pastry to a greased baking sheet and place one fish fillet, skinned side down, in the centre. Spread with the cheese mixture and cover with the second salmon fillet, skinned side up.

Brush the edges of the pastry with a little of the egg. Roll out the remaining pastry and cover the fish. Trim the edges, then pinch them together to seal. Roll out the pastry trimmings and cut them into strips. Brush the top of the pie with beaten egg and arrange the strips in a lattice design over the top. Brush again with beaten egg.

Bake the pie in a preheated oven, 200°C (400°F), Gas Mark 6 for 35-40 minutes, until the pastry is crisp and golden brown. Serve hot with asparagus or courgettes, or cold with a salad.

Potato Tart with Ham, Artichokes and Mushrooms

This free-form tart has a moist, scone-like dough, which is perfect for all sorts of savoury toppings.

Serves 4

75 g/3 oz butter
1 onion, thinly sliced
150 g/5 oz plain flour
125 g/4 oz mashed potato
1 tablespoon olive oil
2 shallots, sliced
125 g/4 oz mushrooms, sliced
125 g/4 oz cooked ham, cut into strips
175 g/6 oz drained canned artichoke hearts, sliced
salt and pepper
thyme sprigs, to garnish

Melt 25 g/1 oz of the butter in a saucepan, add the onion and fry until it is softened and lightly browned. Leave to cool slightly.

Dice the remaining butter and rub it into the flour in a bowl. Add the onion with the pan juices and the mashed potato and season to taste with salt and pepper. Mix to a soft dough. Press out the dough on a prepared baking sheet to a 23 cm/9 inch round. Pinch the edges of the dough to make a rim.

Heat the oil in a frying pan, add the shallots and fry until they are lightly browned. Add the mushrooms and cook briefly until softened.

Scatter the ham and artichokes over the dough, then top with the shallot and mushroom mixture. Season again if wished and bake in a preheated oven, 200°C (400°F), Gas Mark 6 for 25–30 minutes until the pastry is golden brown. Serve hot, garnished with thyme sprigs.

Smoked Salmon and Potato Tart

This unusual tart comprises layers of smoked salmon and cream cheese sandwiched between buttery potato slices.

Serves 6

750 g / 1½ lb boiled potatoes, cooled
65 g / 2½ oz butter, melted
250 g / 8 oz cream cheese, softened
2 tablespoons chopped fresh dill
1 tablespoon lemon juice
1 egg, beaten
125 g / 4 oz smoked salmon, cut in strips
2 tablespoons grated mature Cheddar cheese
salt and pepper

Slice the potatoes very thinly. Grease a 23 cm/9 inch tart tin with a little of the melted butter. Set aside one-third of the potatoes. Arrange the rest in overlapping slices over the base and sides of the tin, brushing each slice lightly with melted butter and sprinkling salt and pepper between the layers.

In a bowl, beat together the cream cheese, dill, lemon juice and egg, with salt and pepper to taste. Spread half the mixture over the potato case and sprinkle with the smoked salmon. Spread the rest of the cream cheese mixture over the salmon.

Top with the reserved potato slices, brush with butter and season as before until the filling is covered. Sprinkle with cheese and bake in a preheated oven, 200°C (400°F), Gas Mark 6 for 35–40 minutes, until the top is brown and crisp.

Sea Bass en Croûte

Serves 6–8

1 kg/2 lb sea bass, skinned and filleted
1 bunch of watercress
25 g/1 oz butter, softened
1 garlic clove, chopped
1 tablespoon lemon juice
500 g/1 lb puff pastry, thawed if frozen
beaten egg, to glaze
salt and pepper

Season the bass fillets on both sides. Trim off any tough stalks from the watercress, wash and dry thoroughly. Plunge the watercress into a saucepan of salted, boiling water and cook for 1 minute, then drain and cool quickly under cold running water. Drain, dry well with paper towels, then chop the watercress finely.

Beat the butter, garlic and lemon juice in a bowl. Season to taste and beat in the watercress.

Roll out half the pastry to measure 2.5 cm/1 inch larger all round than the reassembled fish. Transfer the pastry to a greased baking sheet and place one fish fillet, skinned side down, in the centre. Spread with the watercress mixture and cover with the second bass fillet, skinned side up.

Brush the edges of the pastry with a little of the egg. Roll out the remaining pastry and cover the fish. Trim the edges, then pinch them together to seal. Roll out the pastry trimmings and cut them into strips. Brush the top of the pie with beaten egg and arrange the strips in a lattice design over the top. Brush again with beaten egg.

Bake the pie in a preheated oven, 200°C (400°F), Gas Mark 6 for 35–40 minutes, until the pastry is crisp and golden brown.

Rocky Road Tart

If you want to freeze this tart in advance, cover it closely with clingfilm and foil once the topping has frozen. Put it in the refrigerator for 30 minutes before serving to soften the topping.

Serves 8

150 g/5 oz honey and almond chocolate
1 tablespoon melted butter
75 ml/3 fl oz double cream
450 ml/³/₄ pint chocolate ice cream
450 ml/³/₄ pint strawberry ice cream
450 ml/³/₄ pint vanilla ice cream
100 g/3½ oz mini-marshmallows
50 g/2 oz pecan nuts, roughly chopped
fresh cherries or strawberries, to decorate (optional)

Base:
300 g/10 oz ginger or digestive biscuits
125 g/4 oz butter, melted
50 ml/2 oz honey

Put the biscuits in a plastic bag and tap them with a rolling pin to make crumbs. Mix the butter, honey and biscuit crumbs together in a bowl. Spoon the mixture into a 25 cm/10 inch tart tin, pressing it down into the base and up the sides with the back of a spoon. Chill for 30 minutes.

Put the chocolate, butter and cream into a heatproof bowl above a pan of simmering water until the mixture is melted and smooth. Leave to one side to cool.

Scoop the ice creams on to the biscuit base, alternating the flavours as you go. Sprinkle the top with the marshmallows and pecan nuts. Drizzle the tart with the chocolate sauce and freeze it for 2 hours. Decorate with fresh fruit before serving, if liked.

Chocolate Pear Slice

This quick dessert is smart enough for a special occasion but not too heavy if rich dishes have preceded it. It can be prepared in advance and cooked just before serving.

Serves 6

2 large ripe pears
2 tablespoons lemon juice
350 g / 11 ½ oz puff pastry, defrosted if frozen
150 g / 5 oz plain chocolate, broken into pieces
beaten egg, to glaze
icing sugar, for dusting
pouring cream, to serve

Quarter, core and thinly slice the pears. Put the pear slices in a bowl of water with the lemon juice. Roll out the pastry to a 30 x 18 cm/ 12 x 7 inch rectangle and put on a prepared baking sheet. Use the tip of a sharp knife to make a shallow cut around the pastry, about 1 cm/ ½ inch in from the edges; do not cut right through the pastry.

Melt the chocolate and spread it over the pastry to within 1 cm/½ inch of the cut line. Drain the pears and arrange the slices over the chocolate, keeping them just inside the cut line. Make small indentations on the edges of the pastry with the back of a knife. Brush the pastry edges with beaten egg and bake in a preheated oven, 200°C (400°F), Gas Mark 6 for about 25 minutes until the pastry is risen and golden.

Raise the oven temperature to 230°C (450°F), Gas Mark 8. Generously dust the pastry and pears with icing sugar and return the dish to the oven for about 5 minutes until golden brown. Leave to cool slightly, then serve warm with pouring cream.

Chocolate Velvet Pie

This chocolate shortbread base is an interesting variation on traditional plain shortbread. Swirls of whipped double cream would make a decadent finishing touch.

Serves 10

4 teaspoons powdered gelatine
3 tablespoons cold water
125 g/4 oz caster sugar
3 egg yolks
1 tablespoon cornflour
600 ml/1 pint milk
2 tablespoons finely ground espresso coffee
50 g/2 oz plain chocolate, broken into pieces
chocolate shavings, to decorate

Shortbread
175 g/6 oz plain flour
2 teaspoons cocoa powder
125 g/4 oz unsalted butter, diced
25 g/1 oz caster sugar

Rub the butter into the sifted flour and cocoa powder, add the sugar and mix to a dough. Press evenly over the base and sides of a deep 20 cm/8 inch fluted tart tin. Bake for 20 minutes in a preheated oven, 190°C (375°F), Gas Mark 5 then leave to cool.

Soak the gelatine in water. Whisk the sugar, egg yolks, cornflour and 2 tablespoons of milk. Bring the rest of the milk to the boil with the coffee powder. Whisk it into the egg mixture.

Return the mixture to the saucepan and heat gently, stirring until it thickens. Remove from the heat and beat in the gelatine until dissolved. Add the chocolate and stir until it has melted. Cool slightly then pour the mixture into the tart case. Chill for several hours.

Transfer the pie to a plate and scatter generously with chocolate shavings.

Pear, Wine and Walnut Tart

Serves 6

4 ripe pears
1 tablespoon lemon juice
300 ml/½ pint red wine
125 g/4 oz caster sugar
1 cinnamon stick
4 tablespoons redcurrant jelly
150 ml/¼ pint thick cold custard
150 ml/¼ pint double cream

Pastry:
175 g/6 oz plain flour
75 g/3 oz chilled butter, diced
50 g/2 oz caster sugar
25 g/1 oz walnuts, finely chopped
1 egg yolk
1–2 tablespoons iced water

Sift the flour into a bowl, add the butter and rub in with the fingertips until the mixture resembles breadcrumbs. Stir in the caster sugar and walnuts and add the egg yolk and just enough water to make a firm dough. Roll out the pastry and line a 23 cm/9 inch tart tin. Chill the pastry case for 30 minutes, then bake blind in a preheated oven, 200°C (400°F), Gas Mark 6 for 15 minutes. Remove the paper and beans or foil and return to the oven for 10 minutes.

Peel, halve and core the pears. Brush them with the lemon juice to prevent discoloration. Combine the wine, sugar and cinnamon stick in a saucepan. Bring to the boil, add the pears and poach gently for about 10 minutes until they are tender but still firm. Use a slotted spoon to remove the pears and cinnamon stick from the syrup. Discard the cinnamon. Boil the syrup for about 10 minutes until it is thick and syrupy and stir in the redcurrant jelly.

Brush the inside of the pastry case with a little of the red wine syrup. Whisk the custard in a bowl until it is fluffy. Whip the cream in a separate bowl until stiff, then fold into the custard. Spread the mixture over the pastry case. Slice the pears thinly and arrange them over the filling, then brush with the remaining red wine syrup.

Tarte Tatin

This version of the classic French tart is deceptively simple to make.
Use flavourful, crunchy apples, such as Cox's, and unsalted butter.

Serves 4–6

375 g/12 oz pâte sucrée
50 g/2 oz butter
50 g/2 oz caster sugar
6 dessert apples, peeled, cored and quartered
thick cream or crème fraîche, to serve

Make the pastry (see page 16), wrap it closely in clingfilm and leave it
to chill for 30 minutes.

Melt the butter and sugar in a 20 cm/8 inch ovenproof frying
pan. When the mixture is golden brown, add the apples and toss
them in the syrup to coat them. Cook for a few minutes until the
apples start to caramelize.

Roll out the pastry on a lightly floured surface to a round, a little
larger than the pan. Put it over the apples, tucking the edges of the
pastry inside the edge of the pan until it fits neatly.

Bake in a preheated oven, 190°C (375°F), Gas Mark 5 for
35–40 minutes until the pastry is golden. Leave to cool in the pan for
5 minutes, then put a large plate on top of the pan and invert the tart
on to it. Serve warm with thick cream or crème fraîche.

Lemon and Passion Fruit Pie

In this unusual American pie, the tartness of the lemon tempers the mild sweetness of the yellow-fleshed passion fruit.

Serves 8

375 g/12 oz pâte sucrée
4 eggs
50 g/2 oz sugar
150 ml/¼ pint double cream
finely grated rind and juice of 3 lemons

To decorate
seeds from 3 passion fruit
150 ml/¼ pint double cream, beaten until just holding its shape

Make the pastry (see page 16). Roll it out and line a 20 cm/8 inch fluted tart tin. Chill for 30 minutes, then trim the dough. Bake blind in a preheated oven, 200°C (400°F), Gas Mark 6 for 15 minutes. Remove the beans and paper or foil and return the pastry case to the oven for a further 5 minutes.

Beat together the eggs and sugar, then stir in the cream and lemon rind and juice. Pour the mixture into the pastry case, level the top and bake in a preheated oven, 160°C (325°F), Gas Mark 3, for 25–30 minutes until just set. Leave to cool.

Stir the seeds of two of the passion fruit into the cream, then spoon over the pie. Sprinkle with the remaining seeds and serve within 1 hour.

Mascarpone and Date Tart

The crisp, slightly sweet pastry is a wonderful contrast to the smooth, creamy mascarpone cheese. Fresh dates make an unusual filling.

Serves 8

375 g/12 oz pâte sucrée
250 g/8 oz fresh dates, halved and pitted
250 g/8 oz mascarpone cheese
125 ml/4 fl oz double cream
2 eggs, lightly beaten
2 tablespoons caster sugar
1 tablespoon cornflour
2 teaspoons vanilla essence

Make the pastry (see page 16). Roll out the dough and line a 23 cm/9 inch fluted tart tin. Ease the pastry into the tin, then chill for 30 minutes.

Trim the edges of the pastry case and bake blind in a preheated oven, 200°C (400°F), Gas Mark 6 for 10 minutes. Remove the paper and beans or foil and return the pastry case to the oven for a further 10 minutes. Leave to cool.

Scatter the dates evenly over the base of the cooked pastry case. Combine the mascarpone, cream, eggs, sugar, cornflour and vanilla essence in a bowl and whisk until smooth.

Pour the mixture into the pastry case and bake for 35 minutes, or until the filling is golden and set.

Summer Fruit Flan

Serves 8–10

500 g/1 lb puff pastry, defrosted if frozen
1 egg, plus extra to glaze
50 g/2 oz caster sugar
40 g/1½ oz plain flour
300 ml/½ pint milk
25 g/1 oz butter, diced
few drops of vanilla essence
250 g/8 oz strawberries, hulled and sliced
125 g/4 oz raspberries, hulled
250 g/8 oz cherries, stoned and halved
3 peaches, sliced
125 g/4 oz redcurrants, stemmed
125 g/4 oz blackberries, stemmed
4 tablespoons redcurrant or bramble jelly
a few whole cherries, to decorate

Roll out the pastry to a 30 cm/12 inch square. Put it on a baking sheet, trim a 2.5 cm/1 inch strip from each side and brush the edges with egg. Lay the strips around the edge to form a case, trimming to fit at the corners. Press them down to seal, and pinch the edges.

Prick the base with a fork, brush the edges with egg and bake in a preheated oven, 220°C (425°F), Gas Mark 7 for 20 minutes until the pastry is risen and golden brown. Cool on a wire rack.

Whisk the egg and sugar in a bowl until frothy, then whisk in the flour and 1 tablespoon of milk. Heat the rest of the milk and pour it in. Return the mixture to the pan and cook over a moderate heat, stirring until it is thick and smooth. Off the heat, beat in the butter and vanilla. Cover closely and leave to cool.

Spread the custard over the pastry case and arrange the fruit on top. Decorate with the cherries. Warm the jelly and brush over the fruit and pastry edges. Chill for 2 hours.

Cheesecake Tart with Grand Marnier Berries

Soaking the dried berries in the liqueur not only plumps them up but also ensures that the orange flavour permeates the filling.

Serves 8

175 g/6 oz dried mixed berries and cherries
5 tablespoons Grand Marnier
2 tablespoons clear honey
grated rind of 1 lemon
375 g/12 oz rich shortcrust pastry
250 g/8 oz ricotta cheese
200 g/7 oz cream cheese
100 g/3½ oz caster sugar
3 whole eggs, plus 1 yolk
25 g/1 oz flaked almonds

Put the dried fruit in a small pan with the Grand Marnier, honey and lemon rind. Warm over a low heat until the liquid starts to boil. Remove from the heat, cover and leave until cold.

Roll out the pastry and line a 23 cm/9 inch tart tin. Leave to chill for 30 minutes, then trim away the excess. Bake blind in a preheated oven, 200°C (400°F), Gas Mark 6 for 20 minutes. Remove the paper and beans or foil and return the tart to the oven for 5 minutes.

Beat together the two cheeses, sugar and eggs to make a smooth custard. Stir in half of the dried fruit mixture and pour into the pastry case. Bake for 35 minutes until the tart is firm to the touch and golden on top.

Spoon the remaining dried fruit mixture over the top and top with the flaked almonds. Leave to cool and serve with a glass of Grand Marnier.

Chocolate, Maple and Pecan Tart

This superb tart is similar to a classic pecan pie, but with the addition of a chocolate filling. It's good served warm or chilled.

Serves 8

200 g/7 oz plain chocolate, broken into pieces
50 g/2 oz unsalted butter
75 g/3 oz caster sugar
175 ml/6 fl oz maple syrup
3 eggs
350 g/11½ oz pâte sucrée or puff pastry, defrosted if frozen
125 g/4 oz pecan nuts
icing sugar, for dusting

Melt the chocolate in a bowl over simmering water, then stir in the butter. Put the sugar and maple syrup in a saucepan and heat gently until the sugar dissolves. Leave to cool slightly. Lightly whisk the eggs to a smooth consistency. Whisk in the chocolate and the syrup.

Make the pastry (see pages 16 or 17–18). Roll it out and line a deep 23 cm/9 inch tart tin. Chill for 30 minutes. Pour the filling into the pastry case. Put it on a warm baking sheet and cook in a preheated oven, 190°C (375°F), Gas Mark 5 for 15 minutes until the filling is just starting to set.

Remove the tart from the oven and scatter the pecan nuts over the top. Bake for a further 10 minutes until the nuts are just beginning to brown. Increase the oven temperature to 230°C (450°F), Gas Mark 8.

Dust the tart generously with icing sugar and return to the oven for about 5 minutes until the nuts are beginning to caramelize. Leave to cool for 20 minutes before serving.

Chocolate Swirl Tart

This tart is so easy to make that it will quickly become a firm favourite. The amaretti biscuits add a delicious almond flavour.

Serves 6–8

125 g/4 oz digestive biscuits
50 g/2 oz amaretti biscuits
6 tablespoons butter
200 g/7 oz plain chocolate
250 ml/8 fl oz double cream

Put the biscuits in a plastic bag and crush them with a rolling pin. Melt the butter in a saucepan and stir in the biscuit crumbs. Press the mixture into a greased 23 cm/9 inch pie dish. Chill until firm.

Put the chocolate in a heatproof bowl over a pan of hot water. Stir gently until melted. Cover a rolling pin with foil and brush lightly with oil. Drizzle a little chocolate on to the rolling pin in zigzag lines, about 2.5 cm/1 inch long. Chill until set.

Beat the cream until stiff and fold into the remaining melted chocolate. Spoon into the crumb case and chill for 2 hours until set.

Just before serving, carefully peel the chocolate decorations from the foil and arrange them in the centre of the tart.

White Chocolate and Almond Tart with Mint Cream

Mint and chocolate are the perfect combination of flavours, refreshing and sweet, the one enhancing the other.

Serves 6–8

375 g/12 oz pâte sucrée
125 g/4 oz ground almonds
50 g/2 oz caster sugar
125 g/4 oz butter
2 large eggs
200 g/7 oz white chocolate, finely chopped
25 g/1 oz flaked almonds
25 g/1 oz white chocolate, grated, to decorate

Mint cream
300 ml/½ pint double cream
2 tablespoons chopped mint
2 tablespoons caster sugar

Make the pastry (see page 16). Roll it out and line a 23 cm/9 inch fluted tart tin. Chill for 30 minutes.

Put the almonds, sugar, butter and eggs in a food processor. Blitz until smooth. Add the white chocolate and pulse a few times to mix the chocolate through the mixture.

Spoon the chocolate mixture into the prepared tart case, sprinkle with flaked almonds and bake in a preheated oven, 190°C (375°F), Gas Mark 5 for 40 minutes until the filling is golden and set on top.

Remove the tart from the oven and sprinkle with the grated white chocolate. Whisk together the cream, mint and sugar until thick and serve with the warm tart.

White Chocolate Cherry Tart

Serves 6–8

2 eggs
40 g/1 ½ oz caster sugar
150 g/5 oz white chocolate, finely chopped
300 ml/½ pint double cream
500 g/1 lb fresh black or red cherries, stoned, or 2 x 425 g/14 oz
cans stoned black or red cherries, drained
ground cinnamon, for dusting

Pastry
175 g/6 oz plain flour
½ teaspoon ground cinnamon
125 g/4 oz unsalted butter, diced
25 g/1 oz caster sugar
2–3 tablespoons iced water

To make the pastry, sift the flour and cinnamon into a bowl, add the
butter and rub in with the fingertips. Add the sugar and just enough
water to mix to a firm dough. Roll out the dough and line a
23 cm/9 inch loose-based tart tin. Chill for 30 minutes, then bake
blind in a preheated oven, 200°C (400°F), Gas Mark 6 for 10 minutes.
Remove the paper and beans or foil and return to the oven for a
further 5 minutes.

Beat together the eggs and sugar. Heat the chocolate and cream in
a small bowl over hot water until the chocolate has melted. Pour over
the egg mixture, stirring constantly.

Arrange the cherries in the flan case. Pour the chocolate mixture
over the cherries. Bake in the preheated oven, 180°C (350°F), Gas
Mark 4, for about 45 minutes until the chocolate cream is set. Dust
with cinnamon and serve warm.

Espresso Tart with Chocolate Pastry

This rich, indulgent tart is surprisingly simple to make. For an extra treat, you can decorate the top with chocolate coffee beans.

Serves 8

450 ml/³/₄ pint double cream
3 eggs
125 g/4 oz golden caster sugar
2 tablespoons instant espresso coffee powder
25 g/1 oz dark chocolate, grated

Pastry
200 g/7 oz flour
35 g/1¹/₂ oz good quality cocoa powder
50 g/2 oz golden caster sugar
150 g/5 oz butter, diced
1 large egg, beaten
2–3 tablespoons iced water

To make the pastry, sift the flour and cocoa powder into a bowl. Add the sugar and butter and mix with the fingertips until the mixture resembles breadcrumbs. Add the egg and just enough water to make a firm dough. Roll out the pastry and line a 23 cm/9 inch tart tin. Chill for 30 minutes, then trim the edges.

Bake the pastry case blind in a preheated oven, 200°C (400°F), Gas Mark 6 for 15 minutes. Remove the beans and paper or foil and return the tart to the oven for a further 10 minutes.

Heat the cream until it boils. Whisk the eggs, sugar and coffee powder then pour the hot cream over them, stirring continually. Pour the mixture through a fine sieve and then into the tart case.

Bake for 30–35 minutes or until set. Remove from the oven and sprinkle with grated dark chocolate. Leave to cool before serving.

Praline Choux Tart

Choux pastry doesn't take long to make, but the results always look spectacular. Make this tart for a special occasion. Fresh ripe strawberries are the finishing touch.

Serves 6

500 g/1 lb choux pastry
150 g/5 oz whole almonds, lightly toasted and roughly chopped
150 g/5 oz caster sugar
175 ml/6 oz mascarpone cheese
50 ml/2 fl oz double cream
1 tablespoon icing sugar
3 tablespoons water
fresh berries, to decorate (optional)

Make the pastry (see page 19). Spoon just over one-third of the mixture on to a baking sheet and use the back of a spoon to spread it out into a 23 cm/9 inch disc. Space small spoonfuls of the remaining mixture well apart on another baking sheet. Bake in a preheated oven, 200°C (400°F), Gas Mark 6 for 20 minutes until golden.

Pierce each bun once and the base a few times for the steam to escape. Return to the oven for 5 minutes to dry. If the base is not dry enough give it 5 minutes more. Cool the pastry on a wire rack.

Put the almonds on a sheet of lightly greased foil. Melt the sugar with the water over medium heat until a rich golden colour. Pour over the almonds and leave to cool. Break the praline into pieces. Crush half in a plastic bag with a rolling pin.

Whisk the mascarpone, cream and crushed praline until thickened. Attach the buns around the sides of the pastry base with a little cream. Spoon the rest into the centre of the tart. Dust with icing sugar and decorate the tart with the remaining praline pieces and fresh berries if using.

Crunchy Banana and Pineapple Pie

Serves 6–8

175 g/6 oz ginger biscuits
75 g/3 oz butter, melted
1 banana
200 g/7 oz pineapple chunks, drained if using canned pineapple
375 g/12 oz medium-fat soft cheese
75 g/3 oz caster sugar
1 teaspoon vanilla essence

Crumb the biscuits in a food processor. Alternatively, place them between 2 large sheets of greaseproof paper and crush with a rolling pin. Melt the butter in a saucepan, add the crumbs and stir well. Place 3 tablespoons of the crumb mixture in a small ovenproof dish. Press the remainder over the base and sides of a buttered 20 cm/8 inch pie plate.

Bake the pie case and crumbs in a preheated oven, 200°C (400°F), Gas Mark 6 for 10 minutes until crisp, then leave to cool. Mash the banana with half the pineapple, then mix in the cheese, sugar and vanilla. Spread over the pie case. Pile the reserved pineapple on top and sprinkle with the baked crumbs. Chill until ready to serve.

Mango Star Pie

With its striking star shape, this pie makes a great end to a special meal. Serve with crème fraîche, thin cold custard or pouring cream.

Serves 6

500 g/1 lb puff pastry, thawed if frozen
2 ripe mangoes
2 tablespoons lime juice
50 g/2 oz creamed coconut, grated
25 g/1 oz demerara sugar
beaten egg and caster sugar, to glaze

Roll out half the pastry to a 30 cm/12 inch round. Make V-shaped cuts all round to form a star shape. Roll out the remaining pastry to a 30 cm/12 inch round and place the star-shaped pastry on top. Using a sharp knife, cut the lower piece of pastry to a star shape, using the upper piece as a template.

Peel, halve and stone the mangoes. Cut the flesh into thin slices. Place one piece of pastry on a greased baking sheet and arrange the mango slices on top to within 1 cm/½ inch of the edges. Sprinkle with lime juice, coconut and demerara sugar. Brush the edges of the pastry with water and cover with the remaining piece of pastry. Press the edges firmly to seal.

Brush the top of the pie with egg and sprinkle with sugar. Bake in a preheated oven, 220°C (425°F), Gas Mark 7 for 20–25 minutes, until risen and golden brown. Serve hot.

Crystallized Fruit Flan

Serves 4–6

175 g/6 oz digestive biscuits
75 g/3 oz butter
250 g/8 oz cream cheese, softened
75 g/3 oz caster sugar
1 teaspoon grated lemon rind
4 tablespoons single cream
175 g/6 oz thinly sliced mixed crystallized fruit
icing sugar, for dusting

Crumb the biscuits in a food processor. Alternatively, place them between 2 large sheets of greaseproof paper and crush them with a rolling pin. Melt the butter in a saucepan, add the biscuit crumbs and mix well.

Press the crumb mixture over the base and sides of a loose-bottomed 20 cm/8 inch flan tin. Chill until the base is set.

Beat the cream cheese, caster sugar, lemon rind and cream in a bowl. Carefully transfer the crumb case from the flan tin to a serving plate. Fill the crumb case with the cream cheese mixture, smoothing over the top.

Arrange the crystallized fruit attractively on top of the cream cheese mixture and serve the flan cold.

Chocolate Crumb Tart with Exotic Fruit

Serves 6

175 g/6 oz chocolate digestive biscuits
75 g/3 oz butter
1 tablespoon golden syrup
300 ml/½ pint crème fraîche
selection of exotic fruit, such as pawpaw, pineapple,
pomegranate, star fruit and kumquat
2 tablespoons redcurrant jelly
1 tablespoon lime juice

Crumb the biscuits in a food processor. Alternatively, place them between 2 sheets of greaseproof paper and crush with a rolling pin.

Melt the butter with the syrup in a saucepan. Stir in the crumbs. Press the mixture on to the base and sides of a greased deep 20 cm/8 inch flan tin and chill until firm.

Remove the crumb case from the flan tin and place on a serving plate. Fill the crumb case with crème fraîche then slice the fruit and arrange over the top. Warm the redcurrant jelly with the lime juice in a small saucepan and drizzle over the fruit. Chill the tart for up to 2 hours until ready to serve.

Banoffi Pie

Serves 6-8

175 g/6 oz butter
175 g/6 oz caster sugar
1 x 425 g/14 oz can condensed milk
2 bananas
1 tablespoon lemon juice
150 ml/¼ pint whipping cream
25 g/1 oz dark chocolate, grated

Crumb case
250 g/8 oz digestive biscuits
125 g/4 oz butter

Crumb the biscuits in a food processor or place between 2 sheets of greaseproof paper and crush with a rolling pin. Melt the butter in a pan and stir in the crumbs. Press the mixture evenly over the base and sides of a deep 20 cm/8 inch round flan tin. Chill until firm.

Place the butter and sugar in a pan. Heat gently, stirring until the butter has melted. Stir in the condensed milk and bring to the boil. Lower the heat and simmer for 5 minutes, stirring occasionally, until the mixture becomes a caramel colour. Pour into the crumb base, cool, then chill until set.

Slice the bananas and toss them in the lemon juice. Reserve one-quarter of the bananas for decoration and spread the rest over the filling. Whip the cream and spread over the top. Decorate with the reserved bananas and sprinkle with chocolate.

Just a
Bite

Small tartlets and individual pies make great starters or desserts for elegant meals; they are also perfect for picnics or afternoon tea. Most of the recipes in this book could be scaled-down to make individual portions but the following recipes lend themselves to this special treatment.

Mozzarella and Tomato Tartlets

These tartlets take next to no time to prepare but will make a delicious and filling lunch served with a fresh, crisp salad.

Makes 6

250 g/8 oz puff pastry, defrosted if frozen
beaten egg or milk, to glaze
6 tablespoons sun-dried tomato paste
3 plum tomatoes, deseeded and roughly chopped
125 g/4 oz mozzarella, roughly diced
8 black olives, pitted and roughly chopped
1 garlic clove, finely chopped
2 tablespoons roughly chopped oregano
1 tablespoon pine nuts
olive oil, to drizzle
salt and pepper
mixed salad leaves, to serve

Roll out the pastry to 3 mm/⅛ inch thick. Use a round cutter to stamp out six 12 cm/5 inch discs and put them on a prepared baking sheet. Use a sharp knife to make a shallow mark 1 cm/½ inch in from the edge of each round to form a rim; do not cut right through the pastry. Brush the rims with beaten egg or milk.

Spread 1 tablespoon of tomato paste over each pastry circle. Mix together the tomatoes, mozzarella, olives, garlic, oregano and pine nuts in a small bowl and season to taste with salt and pepper.

Divide this mixture among the pastry circles and drizzle a little olive oil over the tartlets. Bake the tartlets in a preheated oven, 220°C (425°F), Gas Mark 7 for 20 minutes or until the pastry has risen and is golden. Serve at once with mixed salad leaves.

Cherry Tomato Tarts with Pesto

Use ready-made pesto or your own favourite recipe in this colourful dish, but make sure it is green to contrast with the red tomatoes.

Makes 4

2 tablespoons olive oil
1 onion, finely chopped
375 g/12 oz cherry tomatoes
2 garlic cloves, crushed
3 tablespoons sun-dried tomato paste
325 g/11 oz puff pastry, defrosted if frozen
beaten egg, to glaze
150 g/5 oz crème fraîche
2 tablespoons pesto
salt and pepper
basil leaves, to garnish

Heat the oil in a frying pan, add the onion and fry until it is beginning to soften. Halve about 150 g/5 oz of the tomatoes. Remove the pan from the heat, add the garlic and sun-dried tomato paste, then stir in all the tomatoes until they are lightly coated in the sauce.

Roll out the pastry and cut out four 12 cm/5 inch rounds using a cutter or small bowl as a guide. Transfer to a prepared baking sheet and use a sharp knife to make a shallow mark 1 cm/½ inch in from the edge of each round to form a rim; do not cut right through the pastry. Brush the rims with beaten egg.

Pile the tomato mixture on to the centres of the pastry cases, making sure the mixture stays within the rims. Bake in a preheated oven, 220°C (425°F), Gas Mark 7 for about 15 minutes until the pastry is risen and golden.

Meanwhile, lightly mix together the crème fraîche, pesto and salt and pepper in a bowl so that the crème fraîche is streaked with the pesto. Transfer the cooked tartlets to serving plates and spoon over the crème fraîche and pesto sauce. Serve scattered with basil leaves.

Dolcelatte and Broad Bean Tartlets

The inclusion of wholemeal flour in the pastry gives a slightly nutty flavour. Fresh broad beans don't keep well, so use them straight away.

Makes 4

1 red pepper
500 g/1 lb broad beans, in pods
125 g/4 oz dolcelatte, crumbled
2 tablespoons single cream
salt and pepper

Pastry
75 g/3 oz plain flour
75 g/3 oz self-raising wholemeal flour
75 g/3 oz butter, diced
2–3 tablespoons iced water

Mix the flours in a bowl. Add the butter and rub in with the fingertips until the mixture resembles fine breadcrumbs. Add just enough water to make a firm dough. Turn out on to a lightly floured surface, knead briefly and chill for 30 minutes.

Divide the dough into four and roll out each piece to line a shallow 10 cm/4 inch tart tin. Chill the pastry cases for 15 minutes. Prick the base of each tartlet several times with a fork, then bake in a preheated oven, 200°C (400°F), Gas Mark 6 for 15–20 minutes.

Quarter and deseed the pepper, then put the pieces, skin side up, under a hot grill until the skin is charred. Peel off the skin when it is cool enough to handle. Meanwhile, pod the beans and cook in a pan of boiling water for 7–10 minutes until just tender. Drain and skin.

Chop the pepper flesh into small dice, combine it with the beans and divide the mixture among the tartlets. Scatter dolcelatte over the vegetables, then pour over the cream. Season to taste. Bake for 8–10 minutes until the cheese has melted. Serve warm.

Spicy Crab Tartlets

These dainty tartlets are filled with a wonderful combination of
Asian flavours. They are surprisingly easy to make and make
excellent party canapés.

Makes 12

375 g/12 oz shortcrust pastry
125 g/4 oz fresh white crab meat
1 ripe tomato, peeled, deseeded and finely chopped
1 small garlic clove, crushed
2 tablespoons chopped coriander leaves
$\frac{1}{4}$–$\frac{1}{2}$ teaspoon ground cayenne
4 tablespoons mayonnaise
dash of lemon juice
salt and pepper

Roll out the pastry thinly and use a 6 cm/2½ inch cutter to stamp out
12 circles. Line the sections of a bun tin with the pastry, prick the
base of each one with a fork and chill for 15 minutes. Bake in a
preheated oven, 200°C (400°F), Gas Mark 6 for 10–12 minutes until
lightly golden. Leave to cool.

Carefully fork through the crab meat to remove any small pieces
of cartilage that may remain. Add the tomato, garlic, coriander,
cayenne and mayonnaise to the crab.

Add a little lemon juice and season to taste with salt and pepper.
Fill the tartlet cases with the crab mixture and serve.

GARLIC

Filo Tarts with Red Pepper and Pancetta

Makes 6

6 sheets filo pastry, each cut into three 11 cm/4½ inch squares
25 g/1 oz butter, melted
1 tablespoon olive oil
125 g/4 oz pancetta, diced
1 large red pepper, cored deseeded and roughly chopped
1 red onion, roughly chopped
1 teaspoon hot paprika
100 ml/3½ fl oz passata
6 eggs
50 g/2 oz Gruyère cheese, grated

Brush the filo squares with melted butter and stick them together at different angles in piles of three so that you end up with six stacks. Push each stack into a 10 cm/4 inch tart case and bake in a preheated oven, 200°C (400°F), Gas Mark 6 for 8–10 minutes.

Heat the oil in a frying pan and fry the pancetta, red pepper, onion and paprika for 8 minutes until just cooked through. Remove from the heat and stir in the passata. Divide the mixture among the tart cases, making a well in the centre of each tart.

Crack an egg into each well, sprinkle with the cheese and bake in a preheated oven for 20 minutes.

Mixed Mushrooms in Crispy Bread Cases

Makes 8

25 g/1 oz butter
1 shallot, chopped
175 g/6 oz mushrooms (chestnut, oyster, shiitake), sliced
1 tablespoon Madeira
4 tablespoons double cream
1 tablespoon chopped fresh parsley
salt and pepper
assorted salad leaves, to serve

Bread cases
8 thin slices bread, crusts removed
50 g/2 oz butter, melted

Brush both sides of the bread with the butter. Press firmly into 8 tartlet or bun tins. Bake in a preheated oven, 200°C (400°F), Gas Mark 6 for 10–15 minutes, until crisp and golden brown.

Meanwhile, make the filling. Melt the butter in a small saucepan, add the shallot and fry for about 5 minutes until softened. Add the mushrooms and cook for a further 5 minutes, until tender. Stir in the Madeira and allow to bubble briefly, then stir in the cream and chopped parsley, with salt and pepper to taste. Cook over a moderate heat for a few minutes, until the mixture forms a sauce.

Arrange the salad leaves on 8 small plates and place a bread case on each. Fill with the mushroom mixture and serve warm.

Crispy Duck Tarts

These individual tarts have a distinctly oriental flavour partly because of the hoisin sauce, which is a common ingredient in many South-east Asian dishes. Serve hot or cold.

Makes 6

375 g/12 oz puff pastry, defrosted if frozen
beaten egg or milk, to glaze
2 duck legs
6 tablespoons crème fraîche
8 tablespoons hoisin sauce
6 spring onions, thinly sliced
½ cucumber, cut into matchsticks
15 g/½ oz coriander leaves

Roll out the pastry and cut out six 10 cm/4 inch squares. Make two L-shaped cuts in the pastry 2.5 cm/1 inch in from the edge, leaving the two opposite corners uncut. Brush the edges of the pastry square with water. Lift up one cut corner and draw it across the pastry to the opposite cut side. Repeat with the other cut side to form a case. Brush the edges of the pastry with egg or milk, prick the base, put on a prepared baking sheet and chill.

Prick the duck legs with a fork and place on a rack over a baking tin to catch the fat. Roast in a preheated oven, 200°C (400°F), Gas Mark 6 for 30 minutes. Leave to cool, then shred the meat and skin from the duck legs.

Put the meat in a bowl with the crème fraîche and hoisin sauce, mix well and divide among the bases of the prepared tarts. Bake in a preheated oven, 220°C (425°F), Gas Mark 7 for 25 minutes until the pastry has risen and is golden on top.

Mix the spring onion, cucumber and coriander and arrange the mixture on top of the tarts just before serving. The tarts can be eaten hot or cold.

Chicken, Celery and Bacon Tartlets

Makes 8

25 g/1 oz butter
1 celery stick, sliced
2 rindless smoked back bacon rashers, chopped
125 g/4 oz skinless chicken breast, chopped
1 tablespoon sherry
3 tablespoons double cream
1 tablespoon chopped parsley
salt and pepper

Bread cases
8 thin slices bread, crusts removed
50 g/2 oz butter, melted

Brush both sides of the bread with the butter. Press firmly into 8 tartlet or bun tins. Bake in a preheated oven, 200°C (400°F), Gas Mark 6 for 10–15 minutes, until crisp and golden brown.

Meanwhile, make the filling. Melt the butter in a small saucepan, add the celery, bacon and chicken and fry for about 10 minutes until tender and cooked through. Stir in the sherry and allow to bubble briefly, then stir in the cream and chopped parsley, with salt and pepper to taste. Cook over a moderate heat for a few minutes, until the mixture forms a sauce.

Place the cooked bread cases on a serving plate and fill with the chicken mixture. Serve immediately.

Mango Tartlets with Passion Fruit Cream

When you are buying mangoes, choose well-coloured fruit with a shiny, supple skin. Slice downwards, on each side of the large stone.

Makes 4

250 g/8 oz puff pastry, defrosted if frozen
2 ripe mangoes, peeled, stoned and thinly sliced
25 g/1 oz butter, melted
100 g/3½ oz caster sugar
mint sprigs, to decorate

Passion fruit cream
2–3 passion fruit
125 ml/4 fl oz single cream

Roll out the pastry to 5 mm/¼ inch thick and cut out four 12 cm/ 5 inch circles. Put the circles on two prepared baking sheets. Prick the pastry all over with a fork.

Arrange the mango slices on the pastry circles. Spoon the melted butter over the mango slices and pastry and sprinkle the sugar over the top. Bake the tarts in a preheated oven, 220°C (425°F), Gas Mark 7 for 15–20 minutes or until pastry is cooked and golden.

While the tartlets are cooking, cut the passion fruit in half and use a teaspoon to scoop out their pulp into a small bowl. Stir in the cream and mix together thoroughly. Put the tartlets on individual plates and spoon the cream around them. Decorate with mint sprigs and serve immediately.

Strawberry and Almond Tartlets

The almond-flavoured pastry is delicious with a variety of fillings. Try crushed amaretti biscuits mixed with whipped cream and topped with fruit.

Makes 8

250 g/8 oz full-fat soft cheese
1 tablespoon caster sugar
1 teaspoon grated lemon rind
750 g/1½ lb strawberries
5 tablespoons redcurrant jelly, melted
4 tablespoons blanched almonds, toasted

Pastry
250 g/8 oz butter
125 g/4 oz caster sugar
2 egg yolks
375 g/12 oz plain flour, sifted
125 g/4 oz ground almonds

Put the butter and sugar in a bowl and cream until light and fluffy. Beat in the egg yolks. Gradually stir in the flour and ground almonds, and knead to a smooth dough. Cover closely and chill for 1 hour.

Divide the dough into 8 or 16 pieces. Roll out each one into a round to line eight 11 cm/4½ inch or 16 smaller tartlet tins. Bake the pastry cases blind in a preheated oven, 200°C (400°F), Gas Mark 6 for 15 minutes. Remove the paper and beans or foil and return to the oven for a further 3–4 minutes. Leave to cool in the tins on a wire rack.

Beat together the cheese, sugar and lemon rind. Spread a little of the cheese mixture in each pastry case. Reserve 8 or 16 of the best strawberries. Hull and halve the remainder, then put them in the pastry cases.

Spoon the redcurrant jelly over the strawberries and leave to set. Just before serving, top with the reserved strawberries and scatter over the toasted almonds.

Cranberry and Almond Tartlets

Makes 4

300 g/10 oz pâte sucrée
125 g/4 oz softened butter
125 g/4 oz sugar
2 eggs, beaten
125 g/4 oz ground almonds
few drops of almond essence
2 tablespoons plain flour
3 tablespoons cranberry jelly
75 g/3 oz cranberries
icing sugar, for dusting

Make the pastry (see page 16). Divide it into four pieces and roll out each piece to line a 10 cm/4 inch tartlet tin. Prick each base with a fork and chill while you make the filling.

Beat together the butter and sugar until light and fluffy. Add the beaten egg, a little at a time, then add the almonds, almond essence and the flour. Mix well.

Spread the cranberry jelly over the tartlet cases. Divide the almond mixture among the pastry cases and smooth the tops. Arrange the cranberries over the top.

Bake the tartlets in a preheated oven, 200°C (400°F), Gas Mark 6 for 35–40 minutes until the filling is firm. Cool in the tins for 5 minutes, then dust the tops with icing sugar. Serve warm or cold.

Peach and Raspberry Tartlets

These tempting tartlets are simple to make. The tartlet can be cooked several hours ahead, but should be filled just before eating to prevent the pastry going soft.

Makes 4

15 g/½ oz butter, melted
4 sheets filo pastry, each about 25 cm/10 inches square
125 ml/4 fl oz double cream
1 tablespoon soft brown sugar
2 peaches, peeled, halved, stoned and diced
50 g/2 oz raspberries
icing sugar, to dust

Grease 4 deep muffin tins with the melted butter. Cut a sheet of filo pastry in half, then across into 4 equal-sized squares. Use these filo squares to line each muffin tin, arranging them at slightly different angles. Press them down well, tucking the pastry into the tin neatly. Repeat with the remaining pastry.

Bake the filo pastry tartlets in a preheated oven, 200°C (400°F), Gas Mark 6 for 8–10 minutes or until golden. Carefully remove the tartlet cases from the tins and leave to cool on a wire rack.

Pour the cream into a bowl and add the sugar. Whip lightly until it holds its shape. Spoon the cream into the tartlet cases and top with the peaches and raspberries. Dust with icing sugar. Serve at once.

Baked Fig Tarts

Makes 6

400 g / 13 oz pâte sucrée
125 g / 4 oz caster sugar
1 vanilla pod, split
150 ml / ¼ pint orange juice
6 figs
125 g / 4 oz ground almonds
50 g / 2 oz butter
3 eggs, beaten
5 tablespoons plum jam
icing sugar, for dusting
thick cream or crème fraîche, to serve

Make the pastry (see page 16). Roll it out and line a 20 cm/8 inch loose-based tart tin or four individual 10 cm/4 inch loose-based tart tins. Chill for 30 minutes, then bake the pastry blind in a preheated oven, 190°C (375°F), Gas Mark 5 for 10 minutes. Remove the paper and beans or foil and return to the oven for a further 5 minutes.

Cream the butter with 75 g/3 oz sugar and gradually add the beaten eggs. Beat well and then add the ground almonds. Spread the jam over the bottom of the pastry and then spoon the cake mixture over the top. Arrange the figs on top.

Bake for 10–12 minutes for individual tarts or 20 minutes for a large one in a preheated oven or until the sponge has risen and is firm to the touch. Put the remaining sugar in a saucepan with the vanilla pod and orange juice and heat gently to dissolve the sugar, then boil to reduce. Brush over the figs. Leave to cool. Dust with icing sugar and serve with thick cream or crème fraîche.

Banana and Mango Tartlets

Bananas and mangoes give a tropical flavour to these
delicious little tarts, but you could use any combination of your
favourite fresh fruits.

Makes 6

500 g / 1 lb pâte sucrée
6 tablespoons apricot conserve
2 bananas
1 tablespoon lemon juice
1 tablespoon clear honey
1 vanilla pod, split
2 tablespoons double cream
1 small mango
icing sugar, for dusting
mint leaves, to decorate

Make the pastry (see page 16). Roll it out and line six 12.5 cm/5 inch
tartlet tins. Chill for 15 minutes, then bake the pastry cases blind in a
preheated oven, 190°C (375°F), Gas Mark 5 for 10 minutes. Remove
the paper and beans or foil and return the tartlets to the oven for a
further 5 minutes.

Spread the apricot conserve over the bases of the warm pastry
cases. Mash the bananas in a bowl with a fork. Add the lemon juice
and stir in the honey to make a smooth, creamy mixture.

Scrape the seeds out of the vanilla pod, add them to the banana
mixture together with the cream and divide among the pastry cases.

Cut the mango flesh off the stone, peel away the skin and slice the
flesh. Arrange the slices on top of the banana cream. Dust liberally
with icing sugar and serve topped with mint leaves.

Toffee Apple Pecan Tarts

Makes 12

250 g/8 oz pâte sucrée
500 g/1 lb tart green apples, peeled, cored and chopped
1 tablespoon water
50 g/2 oz sugar

Filling
50 g/2 oz butter
50 g/2 oz soft brown sugar
1 tablespoon light corn syrup
50 g/2 oz pecan halves

Make the pastry (see page 16). Roll it out and cut twelve 8 cm/3 inch rounds. Line 12 deep tartlet tins with the dough. Chill for 15 minutes, then bake the pastry cases blind in a preheated oven, 200°C (400°F), Gas Mark 6 for 15 minutes. Remove the paper and beans or foil and leave to cool.

Put the apples in a saucepan with the water, cover tightly and cook gently for about 5 minutes. Remove the pan from the heat and stir in the sugar. If the apple sauce is too liquid, return it to the heat and simmer for a few more minutes. Leave to cool slightly.

Put the butter, soft brown sugar and corn syrup in a saucepan and heat gently, stirring, until the butter has melted, then boil for 2–3 minutes until thick. Remove from the heat and stir in the nuts.

Fill the tartlet cases with apple sauce, then top with a little toffee pecan mixture. Return the tartlets to the oven for 10–15 minutes until bubbling and leave to cool in the tins for 5 minutes.

Lemon Curd Tartlets

Home-made lemon curd is delicious but doesn't keep well, so use some of it up in these little tarts. Alternatively, use a good quality ready-made curd.

Makes 9

500 g/1 lb shortcrust pastry
4 tablespoons lemon curd
250 g/8 oz curd cheese, softened
2 eggs, beaten
50 g/2 oz caster sugar
grated nutmeg, for sprinkling
icing sugar, for dusting

Roll out the pastry thinly and cut nine 10 cm/4 inch rounds. Line a 9 hole muffin tin with the dough, then chill the muffin tin for about 15 minutes.

Put a teaspoon of lemon curd in the base of each pastry case. Mix together the curd cheese, eggs and sugar in a bowl. Divide the filling between the pastry cases and sprinkle with grated nutmeg.

Bake the tartlets in a preheated oven, 200°C (400°F), Gas Mark 6 for 20–25 minutes until the filling has risen and the pastry is crisp. Dust with sifted icing sugar and serve warm or cold.

Chocolate Mousse Tartlets

500 g/1 lb rich shortcrust pastry
175 g/6 oz unsweetened dark chocolate, broken into squares
2–3 tablespoons water
1 tablespoon unsalted butter, diced
1 tablespoon brandy or Cointreau
3 eggs, separated
chocolate shavings, to decorate

Make the pastry (see page 15). Roll it out and line eight 10 cm/4 inch tartlet tins. Reroll the trimmings and line 2 more tins. Chill for 15 minutes, then bake the pastry cases blind in a preheated oven, 200°C (400°F), Gas Mark 6 for 15 minutes. Remove the paper and beans or foil and bake for a further 5 minutes. Leave to cool.

Put the chocolate in a heatproof bowl. Add the water. Set the bowl over a pan of hot water and leave until the chocolate has melted, stirring occasionally.

Remove the bowl from over the water and stir in the butter until it has melted. Add the brandy or Cointreau. Stir in the egg yolks. Beat the egg whites in a clean bowl until they are stiff and dry and fold them into the chocolate mixture.

Spoon the mousse mixture into the tartlet cases, then transfer them to the refrigerator for 2–3 hours until set. Sprinkle with the chocolate shavings and serve cold.

Hazelnut and Summer Fruit Tartlets

Makes 18–20

125 g/4 oz butter, softened
125 g/4 oz caster sugar
125 g/4 oz ground hazelnuts
250 g/8 oz mascarpone cheese
175 g/6 oz strawberries, raspberries or redcurrants

Beat the softened butter and caster sugar in a bowl for 5 minutes until light and fluffy. Beat in the ground hazelnuts.

Grease 2 x 12-hole bun tins. Place a heaped teaspoon of mixture into each. Bake in a preheated oven, 180°C (350°F), Gas Mark 4 for 5–7 minutes or until the mixture has risen up the sides of the tins.

Cool the tartlet cases in the tins for 2 minutes, then remove carefully and cool on a wire rack. Just before serving, fill each tartlet with mascarpone cheese and top with a few pieces of fruit.

Peach Puff Tartlets

These simple but delicious tartlets could also be made with peeled and sliced ripe pear, mango or apple.

Makes 4

250 g/8 oz puff pastry, thawed if frozen
2 ripe peaches, peeled, cored and sliced
25 g/1 oz unsalted butter
4 teaspoons caster sugar
2 tablespoons apricot jam

Divide the pastry into four equal portions and roll each out on a lightly floured surface into a 10 cm/4 inch disc. Space the discs on a greased baking sheet.

Arrange the peach slices on the pastry discs, leaving a narrow border of pastry round the edges. Dot butter over the peach slices, then sprinkle with the sugar. Bake in a preheated oven, 220°C (425°F), Gas Mark 7 for 12–15 minutes, until the pastry is risen and golden and the peach is tender.

Warm the apricot jam in a small saucepan, press it through a sieve into a bowl, then carefully brush over the tops of the tartlets. Serve the tartlets warm.

Apple and Raisin Dumplings

Makes 4

4 cooking apples
1 tablespoon lemon juice
25 g/1 oz demerara sugar
25 g/1 oz butter, diced
50 g/2 oz raisins
½ teaspoon mixed spice
1 egg white, lightly beaten
caster sugar, for sprinkling

Pastry
250 g/8 oz plain flour
125 g/4 oz chilled butter, diced
25 g/1 oz caster sugar
1 egg yolk

Peel and core the apples but leave them whole. Brush them with lemon juice to prevent them discolouring. Mix the demerara sugar, butter, raisins and mixed spice in a bowl and set aside.

To make the pastry, place the flour in a mixing bowl, add the diced butter and rub in with the fingertips until the mixture resembles fine breadcrumbs. Stir in the sugar, then add the egg yolk and enough cold water, about 3–4 tablespoons, to make a firm dough.

Turn the dough out onto a lightly floured surface and knead briefly. Divide the dough into 4 pieces and roll out each to a 15 cm/ 6 inch square. Place an apple in the centre of each and fill the cavities with the raisin mixture.

Brush the edges of the pastry with water, then draw up over the apples to enclose them completely. Place the apples on a baking sheet and brush with the egg white. Sprinkle thickly with caster sugar and bake in a preheated oven, 200°C (400°F), Gas Mark 6 for 40–45 minutes, until the pastry is golden brown. Serve the dumplings hot.

Index

Alaska crumble pie 61
apples:
    apple and raisin dumplings
        125
    tarte Tatin 88
    toffee apple pecan tarts 120
artichokes, potato tart with
    ham, mushrooms and 81
asparagus, Parmesan and egg
    tart 69
aubergine, tomato and haloumi
    tart 23
autumn fruit cobbler 63

bacon: lentil, bacon, spinach
        and Taleggio tart 32
    mushroom tart with smoked
        bacon and thyme 31
    quiche Lorraine 30
baking blind 10–11
banana: banana and mango
        tartlets 119
    crunchy banana and
        pineapple pie 99
    banoffi pie 103
banoffi pie 103
beans: Mexican chilli bean
        tart 34
beetroot and Camembert
    tart 27
broad bean and dolcelatte
    tartlets 108
butternut squash and
    Jarlsberg tart 74

Camembert and cranberry
    pie 40
cheat's rough puff pastry 18
cheese (savoury dishes):
    asparagus, Parmesan and
        egg tart 69
    aubergine, tomato and
        haloumi tart 23
    beetroot and Camembert
        tart 28
    butternut squash and
        Jarlsberg tart 74

Camembert and cranberry
    pie 40
dolcelatte and broad bean
    tartlets 108
dolcelatte and leek galette 68
goats' cheese and cherry
    tomato puff 22
Gorgonzola and hazelnut
    quiche 70
Italian sausage and onion
    tart 35
lentil, bacon, spinach and
    Taleggio tart 32
mozzarella and tomato
    tartlets 106
onion, raisin and pine nut
    tart 78
roast vegetable and feta
    tart 24
sweet potato, chorizo and red
    pepper tart 37
tarte au fromage 26
three cheese puff pie 53
cheese (sweet dishes): lemon
    curd tartlets 121
    mascarpone and date tart 90
    praline choux tart 98
    royal curd tart 57
    strawberry and almond
        tartlets 115
cheesecake tart with Grand
    Marnier berries 92
cherry tart, white chocolate 96
chicory and ham tart 41
chicken: chicken, celery and
        bacon tartlets 113
    chicken pie 45
    smoked chicken and wild
        mushroom tart 79
chilli bean tart, Mexican 34
chocolate: chocolate crumb tart
        with exotic fruit 102
    chocolate, maple and
        pecan tart 93
    chocolate mousse tartlets 122
    chocolate pear slice 85
    chocolate swirl tart 94
    chocolate velvet pie 86
    espresso tart with chocolate
        pastry 97
    rocky road tart 84

white chocolate and almond
  tart 95
white chocolate cherry
  tart 96
chorizo, sweet potato and red
  pepper tart 37
choux pastry 19
coffee: espresso tart with
  chocolate pastry 97
courgettes: courgette and red
  pepper tart 25
  prawn and courgette tart 77
crab tartlets, spicy 109
cranberry and almond tartlets
  116
crystallized fruit flan 101
curd tart, royal 57

date and mascarpone tart 90
decorations, pastry 12–13
dolcelatte and broad bean
  tartlets 108
dolcelatte and leek galette 68
duck tarts, crispy 112

empanadas 47
equipment 6–7
espresso tart with chocolate
  pastry 97

fig tarts, baked 118
filo pastry 11
filo tarts with red pepper and
  pancetta 110
fish pie, crunchy 29
  scalloped 50
fruit flan, summer 91
  crystallized 101

goats' cheese and cherry
  tomato puff 22
Gorgonzola and hazelnut
  quiche 70

ham: butternut squash and
  Jarlsberg tart 74
  ham and potato pie 49
  leek and ham pie 43
  potato tart with ham,
    artichokes and
    mushrooms 81

hazelnut: hazelnut and
  Gorgonzola quiche 70
  hazelnut and summer fruit
    tartlets 123

Italian sausage and onion
  tart 35

leeks: dolcelatte and leek
  galette 68
  Gorgonzola and hazelnut
    quiche 70
  leek and ham pie 43
  leek and mussel tart 78
lemon: lemon and passion fruit
  pie 98
  lemon curd tartlets 121
lentils: lentil, bacon, spinach
  and Taleggio tart 32
  spiced lentil pie 51

mangoes: banana and mango
  tartlets 119
  mango star pie 100
  mango tartlets with passion
    fruit cream 114
mascarpone and date tart 90
Mediterranean salami and
  olive tart 33
Mexican chilli bean tart 34
mozzarella and tomato
  tartlets 106
mushrooms: mixed mushrooms
  in crispy bread cases 111
  mushroom quiche 42
  mushroom tart with smoked
    bacon and thyme 31
  smoked chicken and wild
    mushroom tart 79
mussel and leek tart 78

olives: Mediterranean salami
  and olive tart 33
onions: Italian sausage and
  onion tart 35
  onion, raisin and pine nut
    tart 78
orange and walnut pie 55

pancetta, filo tarts with red
  pepper and 110

passion fruit: lemon and
   passion fruit pie 89
   mango tartlets with passion
      fruit cream 114
pastry: cheat's rough puff
      pastry 18
   choux pastry 19
   decorations 12–13
   making pastry 8–11
   pâte sucrée 16
   puff pastry 17
   shortcrust 14–15
pâte sucrée 16
peaches: peach and honey
      pie 62
   peach and raspberry
      tartlets 117
   peach puff tartlets 124
pears: chocolate pear slice 85
   pear and almond tart 60
   pear and blueberry pie 64
   pear, wine and walnut
      tart 87
pecan nuts: chocolate, maple
      and pecan tart 93
   pecan pie 65
   toffee apple pecan tarts 120
peppers: courgette and red
      pepper tart 25
   filo tarts with red pepper and
      pancetta 110
   sweet potato, chorizo and red
      pepper tart 37
pork and cider pie 38
praline choux tart 98
prawn and courgette tart 77
puff pastry 17
pumpkin pie 58

raspberries: peach and
   raspberry tartlets 117
ratatouille pie 39
rocket, salmon tart with
   wholegrain mustard and 76
rocky road tart 84
root vegetable Tatin 72
rough puff pastry 18
royal curd tart 57

salami: Mediterranean salami
   and olive tart 33

potato and salami tart with
   red pesto 36
salmon: salmon and red pepper
      pie 46
   salmon in puff pastry 80
   salmon tart with wholegrain
      mustard and rocket 76
sardine tart with chermoula 28
sausages: chorizo, sweet potato
      and red pepper tart 37
   Italian sausage and onion
      tart 35
sea bass en croûte 83
shallot tarte Tatin 71
shepherd's pie, crusty 48
shortcrust pastry 14–15
smoked chicken and wild
   mushroom tart 79
smoked haddock and spinach
   tart 75
smoked salmon and potato
   tart 82
steak and kidney pie 44
strawberry and almond
   tartlets 115
summer fruit flan 91
sweet potato, chorizo and red
   pepper tart 37

tarte au fromage 26
tarte Tatin 88
   shallot 71
   root vegetable 72
three cheese puff pie 53
toffee apple pecan tarts 120
tomatoes: aubergine, tomato
      and haloumi tart 23
   cherry tomato tarts with
      pesto 107
   goats' cheese and cherry
      tomato puff 22
   mozzarella and tomato
      tartlets 106
treacle tart 54
turkey, spinach and Brie filo
   pie 52

vegetables: root vegetable
      Tatin 72
   roast vegetable and feta
      tart 24